CLAY CURES

NATURE'S MIRACLE FOR THE NEW AGE

Anjou Musafir
Pascal Chazot

MapinLit
AN IMPRINT OF
MAPIN PUBLISHING

Reprinted in 2020
as Print on Demand

First published in 2006 by
MapinLit
An imprint of
Mapin Publishing Pvt. Ltd
706 Kaivanna, Ellisbridge
Ahmedabad 380006 INDIA
T: +91 79 40 228 228
E: mapin@mapinpub.com
www.mapinpub.com

ISBN: (10 digit) 81-88204-48-X
ISBN: (13 digit) 978-81-88204-48-9
LC: 2006925824

Designed by Paulomi Shah / Mapin Design Studio
Edited by Jayabroto Chatterjee
Illustrations by Gopal Limbad
Printed in United Kingdom

CONTENTS

FOREWORD

The inherent healing qualities of mud were recognized by Mahatma Gandhi, the 'Sleeping prophet' Edgar Cayce, in Indian households, tribes in Africa, in Australia and the people of the Andes Mountains for centuries. Yet, there has been no information that is available for the average citizen. This study by Anjou Musafir and Pascal Chazot will, we hope, contribute towards better understanding and usage of an age-old remedy on the cure of diseases.

The Sarvodaya International Trust, dedicated to the ideas of Mahatma Gandhi, is glad to publish this study by Anjou Musafir and Pascal Chazot and hope it will serve to alleviate many of the problems of ill health.

Mrinalini V. Sarabhai
Trustee, Sarvodaya International Trust

PREFACE

So much of suffering is due to ill health. That there can be a simple, economical and holistic remedy defies all beliefs. Yet this is possible. Treating oneself with clay is an old practice that has been carried out for centuries. Ironically, however, this therapy got lost in the 'reductionist' view of the human body that divides it into particular parts and looks at the symptom but not the cause. Clay treatment, on the other hand, is holistic and helps the body regain its state of health and frees us from the bondage and dependencies created by organised systems.

This book provides practical information about clay and its usage. It also includes experiences in the treatment of illnesses, both personal and those of others, that is authentic and first hand. The narratives are autobiographical in style as we feel that first-hand accounts are more moving than an impersonal third person view.

Mahatma Gandhi, the apostle of non-violence, whose ideologies came to be spread beyond the frontiers of the Indian subcontinent, used clay extensively for curing himself and others around him. A chapter is devoted to his experiences as well.

As we began to write this book, our one-year-old daughter fell ill. She suffered from high fever, cold and diarrhoea. While her fever and illness lasted no more than four days, there was a day when she became completely listless and inert. But at no point in time did we doubt the efficiency of clay. Pascal too was down with a terrible sore throat and cough, losing his voice for a period of time. Our elder daughter was moving around with clay on her arm, as she also suffered from some ailment. Meanwhile, a friend of ours who is a doctor came over to our home around this time. He had diabetes and had heard from us that clay could cure it. Being in the medical profession, he was well aware of the implications. He started with the treatment and stopped any other form of

6	medication. After fifteen days he said he would have to undergo a test under pressure from family and friends. We told him not to expect any miracle in such a short time. He agreed, as fifteen days was really too short a time to cure a grave illness like diabetes.

To our surprise, he called up on the fifteenth day at ten at night and said his sugar level was normal. We were stunned and relieved. Diabetes cured in fifteen days – who has heard of such a thing? Of course, we told our friend to act cautiously and continue with the clay treatment till his erstwhile ailments like gall bladder stones and other complications were cured. Now, two years later, as we finish this book no trace of diabetes has ever resurfaced with him. He is totally cured. Our daughter Tara too has recovered from a terrible skin infection (Impetigo) that consumed half her body and had everyone worried. The aliment had lasted a month, with both of us changing her applications through night and day. Family and friends also pitched in to help when we were away on professional assignments. While the infection was overwhelming, two and a half year old Tara's calmness in her pain was inspiring. She is fully cured today and we have added her affliction to the list of ailments cured by clay applications.

Finally, as the book gets ready to be sent for printing in 2005, we have just seen epidemics rage in Gujarat after a spate of floods, unleashing malaria and the dreaded dengue. Our little Tara contracted high fever (104°F) that lasted four days during which we nursed her with clay applications through night and day. She slept and sipped small quantities of water. By the fifth day her fever returned to normal. However, she suddenly started hallucinating, screaming in terror at imaginary insects and reptiles. She had not slept through the previous night, staring in the dark at the same imaginary creatures. By morning, she appeared to be further gone. We watched helplessly as her little body writhed and she wept and screamed in terror, her lips cracked in dehydration as she refused to drink water any more. The clay application till now was being put on her arm and stomach as she complained of stomach aches. Well-wishers stated that the high fever may have damaged her brain. We were scared and worried. Then, thinking that the fever might have affected her brain, we put a clay cataplasm on her forehead forcibly as she resisted screaming in her fears. The effect was spectacular. Half an hour later, she calmed down and slept. She woke up a couple of hours later, asked to suck ice cubes, began speaking coherently and so began her recovery. A couple of days later, she was back to school. She recovered solely with clay treatment while others around us were hospitalized, under drips and heavy medication. Given the fact that our little girl is less than four years of age, it took a great deal of strength and conviction to fight her disease. The most upsetting and difficult moments were the immense pressures we faced from friends and family to send her to a hospital. Our conviction was often mistaken as obduracy and we were accused of playing with our young child's life and even 'experimenting'. Fighting society's pressures is exhausting and time consuming and those who choose to walk this path must be prepared for this.

We have seen so many miracles with clay that we are irrevocably moved by the great healing power of this simple, modest and ubiquitous but omnipotent substance. The biggest phenomenon was the manner in which it acted on Anjou's father. We have, therefore, devoted an entire chapter to this tragic episode that became a lesson in strength, grace and peace.

We write this book with the conviction that it will relieve many of our physical and mental sufferings. And it is with humility and hope that we share our simple experiences with our readers.

Anjou Musafir and Pascal Chazot

THE ORIGIN OF CLAY AND ITS USE

Earth is older than humanity. Represented as Mother Goddess in several cultures and tribes across the world, the earth has been worshipped as a potent symbol of fertility. In Hindu mythology, Sita comes from the earth and returns euphemistically to its lap at the end of her life's journey. 'Dust to dust' says the Bible. Indeed, earth has been worshipped in many religions and used for its curative powers. Only when we began distancing ourselves from nature did we also start to dissociate ourselves from the earth's therapeutic strengths.

Clay has been in medicinal use since the earliest dawn of medical history. The Egyptians utilized it to mummify dead bodies. Ancient Greeks drew on clay for the treatment of fractures. Discorides of Cilica, who lived around the dawn of the Christian era, describes five kinds of clay in medicinal use in his *Materia Medica*. Galen attributes its discovery to Hermes Trismegistes, the teacher of Aesculapius. Avisenne, the most famous Arab physician (980 to 1039 CE) describes various kinds of clay in medicinal use in his era. In the Middle Ages too there are references to its application for all sorts of complaints like epilepsy and cardiac diseases.

Native Americans used clay extensively for healing and were well aware of its curative properties. Mothers would administer small pieces of clay to their infants in order to pacify them and many consumed edible clay as a dietary supplement or for the purpose of detoxification. Studies of the Inca civilization reveal clay eating as a common practice. In fact, they valued clay more than many other treasures of the empire and, under siege, carried it with them to their secret hideouts.

Improper usage finally led to the decline of clay treatment and it slowly fell into disrepute. It continued to be used in certain parts of the world but more for specific ailments than as a holistic therapy for all diseases.

It is to Dr. Julius Strumpf of Wurzburg that we owe the reintroduction of its use as medication in 1898.[1] His attention to its value was first drawn when, in 1882, he noted that a corpse, which had been buried in clay soil for thirty-seven months and which was then exhumed for medico-legal examination, was in an extraordinary state of preservation. In 1886 he commenced using clay as a paste in the treatment of stubborn septic wounds with most gratifying results. It helped deodorize, protect from irritation and heal. In 1900 Strumpf began orally administering kaolin for the treatment of cholera, dysentery, diarrhoea and septic wounds. He was convinced about the curative properties of clay and went to Dr. Kuhne who was in charge of ailing soldiers belonging to the Serbian armies. These soldiers had been committed to a cholera camp in Bucharest. Dr. Strumpf begged Dr. Kuhne to allow him to treat the cholera patients with kaolin. Terminal patients were handed over to him. The result was astounding. The patients survived and began recovering. As Dr. Strumpf continued with his therapy, the mortality rates dropped from 44 per cent to a mere 3 per cent. It proved far more efficient than other traditional treatments like anti-serum injections, application of iodine etc. Most importantly, it was also easy to use.

After his initial success, Dr. Kuhne went ahead and used clay therapy in all general cases of intestinal disorders. For the treatment of cholera he advocated the following prescription:

Pour 100 gm of finely pulverized clay over 250 c.c of cold water. Shake it until a perfectly homogeneous, creamy liquid is obtained. Administer a tumblerful of this mixture orally to the patient every half hour for six or more doses. After six doses the patient may fall asleep and get over all the acute symptoms. The treatment has to continue with smaller dosage over the next few days, and the patient will be able to leave the hospital within 5 to 10 days. If the administration of the clay preparation orally is difficult, it may be given by an enema each time, with approximately 3 litres of the preparation containing clay.

Kuhne considered all other treatments superfluous and emphasized that for the first eighteen hours after the beginning of the treatment, nothing else should be administered.

Along with German naturopaths Kuhne, Kneipp, Just and Felke who revived an interest in clay as a legitimate therapy, in France Raymond Dextreit's book on clay has been edited in 8 languages and sold more than 980,000 copies in the French language.[2] This is probably the principal reason why one can find purified clay easily in France as compared to many other countries.

Of late, there is a revival of interest in the use of clay for the purpose of cure in many other parts of the world as well. An article on clay eating and detoxification was published by the *American Journal of Clinical Nutrition*. It reported examples of how the Pomo Indians of California sustained themselves despite feeding on bitter, toxic acorns by letting the clay they ate absorb the toxins. The article also mentioned experiments performed on animals that voluntarily ate clay in response to induced poisoning and concluded that clay can adsorb dietary, bacterial and metabolic toxins.

Dr. Benjamin H. Ershoff carried out research sponsored by NASA in order to reverse the effects of calcium deficiency on astronauts. To his surprise he found that calcium supplicants in the diet could not turn around the damage done by osteoporosis. Clay – notably the red desert clay, Terramin, however, produced astonishing benefits on tests conducted on animals. Thus he surmised that clay could induce calcium absorption and help in bone formation.

In India, an older generation of grandmothers and aunts mention the use of *multani mitti* or fuller's earth for skin and hair washes. This tradition still manages to continue as a beauty treatment. In the Saurashtra region of Gujarat we have seen pregnant women eat small tablets of clay. They allow the tablets to dissolve in the mouth, much like a piece of toffee. This helps them obtain minerals that are so essential for their bodies. Inhabitants of the Runjut Valley in the Sikkim Himalayas masticate on red clay as a cure for goitre. This particular variety of red clay is said to be rich in iron.

The *Indian Materia Medica* reports that peasants in some districts use a mixture of clay and vinegar as a cooling local application in fevers. In the treatment of aneurism, in cases of neurosis of the heart and in the cure for disagreeable pulsations of hysteria, clay has been applied with success. A paste of clay smeared to pulsatile tumour not only helped subjective conditions such as asthematic symptoms and cardiac pain, but also aided the objective systems, namely the pulsation and the volume of the tumour and helped diminish the growth, according to Professor Botkin, Dr. Pirogoff and other Russian surgeons. For headaches, pipe clay and ammonium chloride in equal parts made into a paste and applied to the temples gave immense relief.

However, clay therapy by itself is not very widespread. In recent years, nevertheless, interest has been revived in the subject. Dr. Simon Cohen in his book *Calcium Montmorillonite Clay, A Miracle of Life* states:
> In addition to the role it plays as a potent detoxifier, Calcium Montmorillonite Clay has also been used extensively in the treatment of pain, open wounds, colitis, diarrhea, hemorrhoids, stomach ulcers, intestinal problems, acne, anemia and a variety of other health issues. Clay not only cures minor problems such as diarrhoea and constipation through local application, it also acts on all the organs — on the whole organism. Everything unhealthy that emits negative radiations is irresistibly attracted to clay and becomes subject to immediate elimination.

Using clay, earth or mud for curing is not a simple matter of faith or belief. You can be a complete cynic and still be cured! Clay is polyvalent and can cure a wide range of diseases, some acute and some chronic or considered otherwise incurable. We have successfully used only clay on ourselves and our family for treating malaria, diabetes, typhoid, back pains and sciatica, viral fevers, high blood pressure, urinary infections, lung congestions, colds and even after a caesarean section, refusing all other forms of medicines. It has always cured and cured completely. The *Indian Medical Gazatte* confirms:
> Finally, the range of therapeutic application of kaolin is not confined to intestinal disorders and in relieving bleeding from internal organs; it is of value in infantile diarrhoea, as a local treatment in leucorrhoea and in vaginal and uterine inflammation.

The editorial in the *Gazette* goes on to state:
> We have been using kaolin in the treatment of intestinal

disorders for some years, especially in the treatment of bacillary dysentery. Morson's electrically precipitated Osm o-kaolin is probably the best preparation. It may be said that such treatment is exceedingly well tolerated by the patient, is often very successful from a clinical point of view and is a measure of distinct therapeutic value. The usual dose given is 2 drachms suspended in water or milk every 4 hours during the acute dysenteric phase.[3]

There are several other examples of the use of clay (Armenian Bole) in the *Indian Materia Medica:*

When put into the mouth it sticks firmly to the tongue. It is refrigerant, astringent, absorbent and antiseptic. It is used as a powder or paste. Dose is 5 to 30 grains. Internally the powder with cream is given in advance cases of dysentery. A paste made of it in 2 parts, alum 4 parts and rose water 10 in parts is given internally for scalding in the urine. Externally, a paste of it is applied to inflamed and swollen glands; also to ulcers and raw surfaces.[4]

Using clay to cure ourselves implies taking our own health in our hands, becoming conscious of our bodies and assuming responsibility for our actions in the larger context. For example, if you were a smoker, it would be absurd to try clay as a therapy even as you continue to deliberately contaminate yourself with poison. You have to be conscious of your lifestyle, your habits and what you eat. It is a commitment that you must make towards yourself for better health.

Curing oneself also leads to greater autonomy. You free yourself from an external supervisor, advisor or interferer. It implies that you alone know your body and you alone are responsible for it. In your desire to be autonomous and take care of your own health, you exercise the willpower not to fall ill. And, in case you do, your wish to get better goes a long way in restoring and maintaining a state of health.

Gandhiji's Experiences with Clay

Gandhiji was a firm believer in mud therapy and natural cures, and wrote down several of his experiences. He had read Dr. Kuhne's book on nature cure and started to use hydrotherapy, mainly hipbaths. He also discovered the therapeutic properties of clay from Just's book entitled *Return to Nature*, which laid great emphasis on its use. Inspired, he went on to use cold mud poultices on his abdomen to relieve his chronic constipation.

I used to be troubled with constipation and frequent headaches, while at Johannesburg. I kept myself fit with occasional laxatives and a well-regulated diet. But I could hardly call myself healthy, and I always wondered when should I get free from the incubus of these laxative medicines.

... I tried Kuhne's hip baths, which gave me some relief but did not completely cure me. In the meantime, the German who had a vegetarian restaurant, or some other friend, I forget who, placed in my hands Just's *Return to Nature*. In his book I read about earth treatment ... The treatment consisted in applying to the abdomen a bandage of clean earth moistened with cold water and spread like a poultice on fine linen. This I applied at bedtime, removing it during the night or in the morning, whenever I happened to wake up. It proved a radical cure. Since then I have tried the treatment on myself and my friends and never had reason to regret it.[5]

For constipation, Gandhiji recommended a mud poultice three inches broad, six inches long and half an inch thick for application on the lower abdomen. Mud therapy helped rid him of his dependence on fruit

14   salts. He also strongly advocated the application of mud poultice to the head for headaches and fevers, stating that as a general rule it provided relief. He used clay for wasp stings and scorpion bites, and even in severe cases of typhoid. He writes that there were nearly ten incidents of typhoid fever in Sevagram. Mud therapy provided complete recovery in every case, with the result that the inmates of the Ashram were no longer afraid of typhoid fever. For boils and abscesses, he would dip a piece of cloth in a solution of potassium permanganate and then pack the mud inside it. In fact, he says that he did not remember a single case in which this cure failed. Gandhiji wrote, 'Hot mud poultices (can be used) as a substitute for anti-phlogistine. A little oil and salt is added to the mud and it is heated sufficiently long to ensure sterilisation'.[6]

He utilized mainly sweet smelling clean red earth. He also used clay or earth as he called it, for treating the fractured arm of his third son Ramdas. They were on a boat to South Africa and, while playing with the Captain's son, Ramdas landed his arm in a sling. With his characteristic candidness, Gandhiji wrote in *Nature Care*:

> He was just eight years old. I asked him if he would not mind my dressing his wound. With a smile he said he did not mind at all. It was not possible for him at that age to decide what was the best thing for him, but he knew very well the distinction between quackery and proper medical treatment. And he knew my habit of home treatment and had faith enough to trust himself to me. In fear and trembling I undid the bandage, washed the wound, applied a clean earth poultice and tied the arm up again. This sort of dressing went on daily for about a month until the wound was completely healed. There was no hitch, and the wound took no more time to heal than the ship's doctor had said it would.

Most people who use nature cure methods on their own children are often under tremendous pressure from society. They are accused of taking risks. It is important to point out that as with Gandhiji, experiments with our own body comes first, before we can make choices for our children. No sane individual should start on naturopathy after having heard or read about it. In any case, deep conviction comes from one's own experiences. Be prepared for taunts, jibes and comments from friends and family! Gandhiji's autobiography also mentions the remarks of friends who suggested he was callous and dogmatic and that he should have sought the help of a doctor. At one point, even Gandhiji wavered under pressure. But his own experiences strengthened his convictions and, ultimately, he did not succumb. Gandhiji was certainly a strong believer in nature cure.

Allopathic drugs lull an individual into a false sense of security. While most people feel they are cured, the drugs mostly repress the disease. When we pop in a painkiller for a headache, the relief is only temporary. The root cause of the ache does not disappear. That is why holistic and natural treatments go a long way in dealing with the problem from the source and curing us completely.

Gandhiji had very strong views on the medical system and profession. He wrote:

Doctors have almost unhinged us. Sometimes I think that quacks are better than highly qualified doctors. Let us consider: The business of a doctor is to take care of the body, or, properly speaking, not even that. Their business is really to rid the body of the diseases that may afflict it. How do these diseases arise? Surely by our negligence or indulgence. I overeat, I have indigestion, I go to a doctor, he gives me medicine, I am cured. I overeat again, I take his pills again ... I have indulged in vice, I contract a disease, a doctor cures me, the odds are that I shall repeat the vice. Had the doctor not intervened, Nature would have done its work, and I would have acquired mastery over myself, would have been freed from vice and would have become happy ... Hospitals are institutions for propagating sin ... It is worth considering why we take up the profession of medicine. It is certainly not for the purpose of serving humanity. We become doctors so that we may obtain honours and riches ... Doctors make a show of their knowledge and charge exorbitant fees.[7]

If allopathic drugs could cure, then why does an individual get the same illness or disease again and again? A case in point is malaria. Once one starts taking medicines, one continues with stronger doses each time and this makes the body weaker and more dependent on drugs. As the body becomes resistant to drugs, so does the parasite, bacteria or virus. Mosquitoes are known to have mutated as a reaction to the heavy doses of quinine present in the body of human beings.

The following passage provides interesting information on the progress of medicine and its impact on human health.

> We are healthier today not so much because we are receiving better treatment when we are ill, but because we tend not to become ill in the first place. The main effect of many advances is that people are now able to live longer with their illnesses.
>
> Modern medicine acts as all health problems are biological and can ultimately be solve through research. But the diseases that threaten us now are very different from those infectious diseases against which medicine has proved so successful. Now the main threats are degenerative diseases such as heart disease, cancer, rheumatoid arthritis, osteoporosis and diabetes, and those associated with the breakdown of the immune system such as AIDS . . .
>
> Nature also keeps pace with our medical ingenuity. As fast as we develop drugs to cure infections, the micro-organisms change and adapt. For example, pneumonococcus is a bacterium responsible for meningitis, pneumonia and middle ear infections. Research at the American Centre for Disease Control and Prevention in 1955 found that 25 per cent of patients were infected by a strain of pneumonococcus that was resistant to penicillin. Ten years earlier, in 1985 the frequency of penicillin-resistant pneumonococcus was less than 1/10 of 1 per cent.
>
> A survey of half the intensive care units in Europe carried out by the *Journal of American Medical Association* found more than 20 per cent of the patients they

examined had infections which were acquired in the unit. These infections were resistant to antibiotics. A three-week stay in intensive care increases your risk of infection 33 times. As fast as we find drugs, micro-organisms become resistant to them.

Medicine has less impact on our health than we think and we have more influence than we give ourselves credit for. This is clear when doctors are not available. In 1973, when doctors in Israel were on strike for a month, admissions to hospitals went down by 85 per cent. The death rate dropped by 50 per cent to reach its lowest recorded level. The previous low level was 20 years before – also during a doctors' strike. During a doctors' strike in Los Angeles County in 1976 to protest against high malpractice insurance premiums, the death rate fell by nearly 20 per cent. Sixty per cent fewer operations were performed. At the end of the strike the death rate quickly rose to normal levels. Such strikes bring home that your *individual* longevity and *individual* health are your responsibility.[8]

The French doctor, Jean Valnet, writes how antibiotics have become habit forming. During the Second World War, antibiotics saved the lives and limbs of thousands. Valnet narrates that one evening, after the Battle of Colmar, they received more than 400 injured soldiers. He rushed to Strasbourg during a freezing night in an uncomfortable jeep and exhausted drivers to bring back some penicillin. Upon his return, he got together ten million units of penicillin with the help of which he was able to save more than a hundred soldiers with 100,000 to 200,000 units injected for every patient. Today, he writes, a patient is injected with several million units per day for a period of three to twenty days. And these injections are given for common colds or laryngitis that can be cured with natural essences of eucalyptus, cinnamon, cloves etc. within a period of twenty-four to forty-eight hours or a maximum of eight days!

For those who are injured or operated upon, he continues, it is now habitual practice to systematically administer them several millions of units of penicillin every day along with other drugs such as Terramycin,

Streptomycin or other antibiotics. Valnet then quotes an American doctor who asked for a ban on antibiotics, stating that the post-operative infection in patients not injected with antibiotics was a mere 1.3 per cent compared to the 4 per cent in those injected with high doses of antibiotics.[9]

Valnet gave these figures in 1976. The amount of antibiotics used to save an injured battalion in the 1940s was already routinely administered daily to one human being for several days for common diseases in the 1970s. Today, several decades later, the use of antibiotics and its dependency is much more alarming.

Naturopathy, on the other hand, is a different vision of the world and of the human body. Allopathy studies illness. Naturopathy studies health. More elaborately, in the present system of allopathic medicines, one studies the symptoms of the illness. This does not take into account the individual.

Naturopathy studies the state of health and how best to remain in that state of health. This is a profound point of view. Naturopathy respects your body, remaining in tune with it and maintaining harmony with the universe at large. Gandhiji wrote:

> The Nature Cure man does not 'sell a cure' to the patient. He teaches him the right way of living in his home, which would not only cure him of his particular ailment but also save him from falling ill in future. The ordinary doctor or vaidya is interested mostly in the study of disease. The Nature Curist is interested more in the study of health. His real interest begins where that of the ordinary doctor ends; the eradication of the patient's ailment under nature cure marks only the beginning of a way of life in which there is no room for illness or disease. Nature Cure is thus a way of life.[10]

It is largely accepted that illnesses are the result of accumulated toxins in the body. There are several ways of eliminating them. The easiest way is using clay.

MY EXPERIENCES WITH CLAY

Anjou Musafir

HOW I DISCOVERED CLAY

Like most people who surround me, I too was a sceptic when it came to using clay for healing. The first time I learnt about clay was through my husband Pascal. We were not married at that time. In fact, I was a teacher at Alliance Française in Ahmedabad (India) and in 1990 he was posted there as Director. Pascal was very passionate about the therapeutic use of clay and what he said about allopathic drugs and doctors, in general, is summarized in Gandhiji's quote in the previous chapter.

At that time I thought Pascal was another *firangi* – a typical foreigner – trapped inevitably in the frills of oriental mysticism. He was rabid about avoiding onion, garlic and tomato in his vegetarian meals and often examined his food closely with a fork every time we ate out. I wondered whether his fanatic attitude was merely part of his personality that bordered on the extreme. In fact, secretly, I thought him to be a bit misguided about the curative properties of clay. As I was often sick, his tirades went on but I listened with a good deal of humour and cynicism.

I had also witnessed Pascal's spectacular and miraculous recovery from Bell's Palsy with the help of clay therapy. Nevertheless, I remained a passive observer. I guess it is only when you use the cure properly and with conviction (when the situation is desperate) that it works. I did use it once when I had a cold. I put it on my nose – a most inconvenient spot – tried to wear my spectacles and watch a film to pass time. The clay ran all over my face and I thought I looked straight out of a horror film! After managing to keep it on for thirty long minutes, I hurried to wash it off. Needless to say, it had no effect and I was even more convinced that clay could not cure.

URINARY INFECTION

In 1994 I picked up a severe urinary infection. The lady doctor I had hurried to informed me in a matter of fact manner that many young girls suffered from this malady. I was given a full course of antibiotics and other drugs. This gave me blisters in my mouth, along with other side effects. As the days went by, my infection became worse and so painful that I could hardly move. The doctor then prescribed anti-inflammatory tablets. This too did not soothe my pain. To make matters worse, I developed rigors and started shivering and shot up a high fever. In the past, as I had often suffered from bouts of cerebral malaria that was quite rampant in our city, the doctor – a new one this time – prescribed Lariago tablets even before making me go through a blood test. I am told that many doctors did this as a preventive measure. In a matter of a few hours I was vomiting and soon I began to have strange fears. I could not even retain a drop of water. The pain was agonizing and my fever-ridden body was racked with spells of relentless shivering. The doctor calmly told my mother that I should now be given Lariago intravenously. That, I think, was the last straw. Coming from a doctor who was also a most disagreeable neighbour, it didn't make sense to me to put myself through further torture. Surely I could not put such a callous man in charge of my body! I suddenly remembered Pascal's words. He had told me time and again that I should listen to my body. I now realized that it could not tolerate these medicines and was trying to find a way to throw them out. Should I still insist on letting them poison me? I made up my mind instantly and stopped having the medicines.

In great pain and perhaps in sheer desperation I took some clay and soaked it. As soon as it appeared to be ready, I put it on a long strip of cloth and tied it on my stomach. The immediate effect was cooling and pleasant. Within twenty-five to thirty minutes I began to feel the difference. My pain eased and an hour later, I was moving around feeling much relieved. I could not believe it. How did it ease my pain and so fast, I wondered. If I doubted its efficiency, in three hours' time, when the effects had worn off, the excruciating pain returned to remind me of my earlier suffering. That is when I knew for sure that it was the clay that had helped alleviate my agony. From that moment I started on clay therapy in earnest. I think it went on for a fairly long time – several weeks, in fact. I went to work with clay in a pot and strips of cloth smothered with the miracle medicine strapped to my body that I changed throughout the day and

night. I did not have to look at the time or keep an alarm clock. Even at
night I would wake up, realizing that the clay was quite dry and needed to be changed.

I was cured in a few weeks but a year later, when my father was hospitalized, I got a fresh attack. I am sure it was due to the shock of my father's precarious condition. This time the assault was severe. Wherever I went – whether to the hospital or to teach – I always carried the clay with me. This time the infection lasted a month. I remember getting fed up of all the discomfort that came with changing the clay strips and lugging around the pot. When would I get cured, I would ask myself in anger. If I stopped the treatment or had gaps between each application, the pain returned. The process seemed interminable!

I removed the application after nearly a month. The memory is still clear in my mind. As I unwrapped the cloth, I strongly felt I did not need to put a fresh application again. I was sure I was cured. And I was. It is amazing how I knew that I was rid of the infection. It was the beginning of the process of becoming in tune with my body.

A couple of years later I was married to Pascal in 1995. I was studying at the University in Paris, appearing for my exams in a language that was not my native tongue. It was winter and bitterly cold, perhaps the coldest in years. I was stressed, coping with the dark, grey skies and hoping that my style of expression in French would hold me in good stead. I was lucky that I had an abundant supply of good *argile verte* or green clay that is available in the medical shops. The infection returned and lasted around fifteen days. The very last time was on a vacation in Thailand. Remaining the whole day in a nylon swimming costume could have brought it on. However, this time it did not linger long. And then it was goodbye forever! It has been many years now and I am sure I will not get it again. So many girls suffer from this malady that is recurrent and painful. Using clay, I am convinced, will help them too, provided they use it properly and maintain good hygiene.

MALARIA
I had been suffering from recurrent bouts of malaria that became rather frequent by the time I was twenty-six years old. As I mentioned

earlier, I am not sure whether I also had malaria when I contracted the urinary infection. At any rate, I had always been given allopathic medicines.

After our marriage in India I went to live in Pascal's home in Ahmedabad. It was immense but, alas, severely mosquito-infested. There were dark corners around the old wooden sculpted doors Pascal had collected. Green plants and creepers and lack of sunlight in some places made it fit for mosquitoes to adopt it as their palatial residence. As Pascal's non-violent philosophy did not permit anyone to use repellents except those of the herbal variety that did not kill, it was a foregone conclusion that I would contract malaria within days of my wedding. I had high fever and bouts of shivering. I applied clay on my forehead as that felt most comfortable. The crisis lasted three days. By the end of the third day my fever had gone. On the fourth day I was up and about. It has been nearly eight years since then. I have never again contracted malaria, though I continue to live in the same city and am often bitten by mosquitoes. My body has developed its own immunity with the help of clay therapy.

Pascal had also once contracted malaria. He cured himself with clay and though he has been staying in Ahmedabad for these past twelve years, he has never caught it again. His daughter Lissa too had an attack of this dreaded fever when she was about eleven. Her temperature shot up to 104° F for about three days. But she remained calm and took care of herself with the help of clay therapy. During the period of her illness, we had to sometimes leave her alone in that large house for short periods of time due to our prior commitments. Lissa was quite autonomous. She was not only all right after four days, but had a new lease of energy and joined school immediately. Needless to say, she too has never had malaria again.

MIGRAINE

Ever since I can remember I have suffered from headaches. My mother took me to all sorts of specialists when I was young and living with my parents in New Delhi. The specialists had different opinions. Some felt it was due to my poor eyesight; others put the blame on my inflamed sinus. But opinion remained divided.

When I was in college I started getting migraines so often and for
such long periods that I found I was forced to take stronger drugs day by
day. The attacks lasted several days. I also tried homeopathy, which
provided some relief but the minute I stopped the medication, the
headaches returned.

I recall one such severe spell. By then I had started to use clay
quite adeptly. When I got the attack, I put clay on my forehead straight
away. But the application provided no immediate relief like it normally
does. There were hammers beating in my head and it was absolutely
unbearable. I asked Pascal what was the matter. He told me to try putting
the clay on another area. I asked him where. He said that ultimately I
would have to figure out and understand my own body. However, he
suggested I try applying clay over the spot where I had my liver. I did as he
had advised and the results were spectacular. I vomited in minutes and my
headache subsided immediately. As a twenty-seven year old at that point
in time, it was the first occasion I realized that my headaches were not
due to my poor eyesight or sinus but because of a weak liver, aggravated
by bouts of overeating, especially my mother's delicious food. I proceeded
to detoxify my liver by applying clay on it. I am glad to say that I am cured
of my migraine now, except when I binge!

SCIATICA
I have also suffered a weak back. Sometimes the pain down my
lower back could be excruciating. I knew Sciatica was the culprit. For relief
I would do some Yoga *asanas* that helped. But I was unable to continue
with them due to my erratic work schedule. So, when I was down with an
attack, I simply applied clay on my lower back. This not only provided
immediate relief but, thankfully, also cured me over a period of time. Now I
get the pain only when I exert myself by carrying anything heavy. And a
couple of applications are all that I need at night to get back into action!

When Pascal was Director of the Alliance Française, a neighbour
in our office compound complained that she had sciatica and was
perpetually bed-ridden. Her interest in alternative therapy started her on
clay treatment. She was advised to put clay along the path where the
sciatic nerve ran. Pascal had warned that there might be a reaction. If
there was not, then she could try putting the clay on her lower back as

well. A few days later, when asked how she was feeling, she mentioned she had found great relief from her pain, but had developed some boils along her leg. Pascal asked her whether she had any other disease. She revealed she also suffered from diabetes for which she was taking medication. Pascal asked her to continue with the clay applications as her body had found an outlet. She followed Pascal's instructions and a few weeks later said that her blood sugar had returned to normal and, therefore, she no longer needed to take the medications. Pascal asked her to just continue with the clay treatment. She did so and her sciatica was cured, which had always been her desire. The clay only had one side effect — it cured her of her diabetes as well!

DIABETES

So many people suffer from this illness and it is, indeed, a pity that many patients have to spend the rest of their lives entirely dependent on drugs and injections. My father was a big-built, six foot tall Sikh. He rarely fell ill. Nevertheless, for no apparent reason, when he started to feel faint and rapidly lose weight, he went for a check up. His blood sugar was detected at an all-time high, with the count soaring to a dizzy 500. We were told that patients go into a diabetic coma when the sugar count is above 300. My father's robust constitution saved him from collapsing. He was prescribed the usual drugs. He returned thoroughly disheartened, as he never liked depending on medicines. I suggested he try clay therapy. He was very amenable to the idea and began the treatment in earnest. We used *multani mitti* at that time. He applied it on his arm day and night. But he also went to work, drove a hundred kilometres to his factory at Limbdi and attended meetings with his applications of clay intact! In a month's time his blood sugar started to come down and within three months it was back to normal. He continued some more time thereafter and his subsequent tests revealed he had been definitely cured.

This may not be a common occurrence. It is largely believed that the sugar count can be controlled but that the diabetic condition can recur. When my father was hospitalized in an emergency situation (see next section), he was given bottles of glucose. The neurosurgeon asked whether he had any history of any other disease. We told him he had had diabetes and that he had been cured. The doctor panicked because he knew glucose would be fatal to a diabetic patient and, moreover, my father was also suffering from trauma and internal haemorrhage. My poor father was subjected to another round of tests and to their immense surprise, it showed his blood sugar as normal. A friend, who was a specialist in diabetes and often came to give him a check-up, revealed his total amazement and, later, at a national seminar mentioned how my father had been cured with clay therapy.

A GREAT TRAGEDY

I write this to share one of the most painful experiences of my life that became a lesson in strength and faith. My father was alone at home and had a terrible accident. He had been suffering from depression. He was also under some prescribed psychiatric drugs, though at that time I was not aware of this fact. What he did in a moment of weakness we shall never know. Spurred by a powerful intuition, my mother suddenly felt that something terrible had happened. Both she and I were at my residence not far from theirs. We rushed back, broke open the door to find him lying in a pool of blood, a rifle next to him. With some help, we managed to rush him to the civil hospital. I skip the details of the callous attitude of some of the local staff that is, alas, routine in many government hospitals. By the time we pulled strings to get some good doctors to attend on him, we were told that he had a bullet lodged in his brain and that his case was too complicated. He was in a coma, suffering from internal haemorrhage. His face was swollen beyond recognition. The neurosurgeon confessed that only a miracle could save him. If he survived for the next twenty-four hours, only then could some blood clots be removed. But this seemed a remote possibility.

Pascal told me that if something could save him, it would have to be clay. We should not waste a minute, he advised. In a state of shock, everything seemed like a nightmare in slow motion. But I rushed home and got the *multani mitti* or yellow clay that was ready. Returning to the hospital, I applied a good deal straight on his forehead. I then sat next to him and spoke to him gently, asking him to fight back. I told him all of us loved him dearly. And I prayed. I prayed that his good deeds stand by him. And I prayed he should leave this world not in such a violent manner but in a more peaceful state. I changed the clay continuously throughout night. Within twenty-four hours his face became normal. All the swelling disappeared and he looked as if he were sleeping.

It was obvious that it would be impossible to operate on him and remove the bullet. The X-ray reports showed its presence quite clearly. The inside of his mouth had a hole made by the passage of the bullet.

Days merged into endless nights. In the midst of a stream of well-wishers and family members, I continued stoically with the clay applications. A few eyebrows were raised among the visiting junior doctors. I pretended this was a religious rite. No questions were asked thereafter. My father's internal injuries, including those in his mouth, healed completely without any surgery, stitches or medication. Soon my father was moved from the ICU. Now I was witness to more suffering, pain and death all around me in the general ward.

My father remained in a coma. I continued with the clay applications, uninterrupted, and I also continued to pray. Next to his bed lay a young man. He too was in a coma due to a head injury caused by a fall from a scooter into an open manhole. The fact that he was unconscious for the past six months was hardly reassuring.

One day, exactly a month after his accident, as I sat by his side, my father suddenly opened his eyes and looked at me. He had slipped out of his coma! Soon he started to talk, though it seemed apparent that he had lost his memory. With the loss of his memory away went all his suffering. After all, memory is suffering. What a blessing! Purity and tenderness shone from his eyes. In a short while, he was able to leave the hospital and return home. Neither his face nor his body bore any physical traces of the wounds or the trauma. He looked handsome and healthy. Due to the continuous applications of clay, his skin had improved and so had his hair.

In the months that followed, he began to walk with help. He was able to recall with association names and addresses. I struggled to continue with the clay applications. I knew people remained sceptical. But it was not my intention to make them believe in clay therapy. I only hoped they would carry on with the treatment in my absence, when I was away at work. Then, a few months later, I left for France on a scholarship. I was to be away for a month. I left strict instructions with the nurse and my family members to ensure that the clay treatment did not stop. My last impression of my father, as I was leaving home, was seeing him dancing with my mother to *Lara's Theme* from his favourite film, *Dr. Zhivago*.

A week later, in France, I was shocked to learn that he had suffered some fits and was taken back to the hospital in a coma. This time he was under heavy medication. His feet had swollen due to injections. I was asked to return as his condition turned serious. Questioning several members of my family over the phone, I learnt that his clay applications had been discontinued. Anger welled inside my heart. I had left my father on the road to recovery with entreaties to those who were to care for him that they continue with the clay treatment even if they did not believe in it. I furiously insisted that they immediately restart it. They did. Within a week he was out of his coma for the second time. However, he returned home with some kind of paralysis of the throat. As he could not eat or swallow, the doctors put a tube through his mouth to feed him. When I returned to Ahmedabad, I realized how painful the tube must have been.

Again, I had to be adamant so that his caregivers put clay on his throat. One of them objected that he would die of a cold! Finally, putting all resistance aside, we went ahead with the clay therapy. A week later, while we were sitting near him, suddenly he started pulling out the tube from his mouth. My mother panicked. Pascal said she needed to be confident with him because my father knew what he is doing. Having removed the entire tube, he sat quietly. My mother rushed out and reappeared with a tray of water, *parathas* and fruit, in keeping with her Punjabi genes. She deposited the tray in front of him. My father, not to be outdone, remained true to *his* Punjabi genes as well. He picked up the glass of water with trembling hands and drank it. Then, to our utter surprise, he ate the food that lay on the tray. He was cured once again!

This time, however, his second hospitalization had attacked his body. His recovery was slower. He was no longer able to walk. A year later he fell sick. His fever was abnormally high and diagnosed as malaria. My father lived in Limbdi, a hundred kilometres away from us. In my absence, a local doctor gave him several injections but his fever did not subside. When I learnt about this, I insisted he be brought to Ahmedabad. And when I saw him, I realized that the medication had taken its inevitable toll. He was weak and riddled with very high fever. My mother wished again that he be hospitalized. I resisted since I knew how much my proud father hated hospitals and medications. I nursed him day and night, changing the clay and sponging him. He had stopped eating and continued to sleep. Three days later, in the afternoon, I felt nervous and called Pascal who was in his office. We sat around him – my mother, Pascal, our elder daughter, Lissa, my maternal uncles and I. Deep in my heart I prayed that he be released from his suffering. I was prepared. Perhaps, so was he. Quietly exhaling his last breath, he bid us a final goodbye in our arms. He had died in his own home, on his own bed, surrounded by those he loved. His karma did not let him down. And my prayers were answered.

We completed the last rites on the same day. My mother and I did not wish his body to deteriorate. He looked so handsome and peaceful that no one could have guessed how much he had suffered. He went like a proud soldier, amidst the chanting of hymns. Contrary to tradition, I, his daughter, lit his pyre. And in that moment of life's greatest truth, I realized that though any ailment can be cured with clay, we are ultimately mortal.

MY PREGNANCY AND CAESARIAN SECTION

I had the most wonderful time during my entire pregnancy. Since I was carrying my first baby when I was thirty-four years old, I had the usual dose of largely pessimistic advice. I had been using clay earlier and as a result of that, I had no morning sickness. In fact, I simply felt on the top of the world! Perhaps a lot of women feel that way when they are expecting a baby.

I'd like to point out that I had always had a very delicate constitution, suffered a great deal of illnesses when I was a child, and from what my mother tells of me, must have created hell for her when I was an infant. That may have been one of the reasons why I had hesitated so long before deciding to have a baby.

By the time I got pregnant, I had been using clay for more that eight years. I felt energetic and happy. In fact, I had a good deal of stamina and continued working well into my eighth month, all the while climbing three floors of steps to my apartment. I even went to France and spent an active month there, walking long distances, climbing the flight of stairs old Parisian apartments are famous for and hopping in and out of the metro. All I took were some natural Ayurvedic supplements. I also drank some clay from time to time. For this, I used the French green clay, which is purified. Too much walking all over Paris did gave me a few excruciating backaches. But, undaunted, I would apply clay and bounce back to my feet!

In the meanwhile, the big question remained unanswered. Where would I give birth to my baby?

We were sure that it would have to be at Ahmedabad in India. As soon as I returned, I went around looking for lady gynaecologists. Two conditions needed to be fulfilled. One was that I wanted an all-women team. No male doctors! This was not just a superficial feminist demand. It had to do with my profound conviction in the healing powers of women. If anyone has read Groddeck's *Le Livre de Ca,* they will understand what I mean. Anyway, I did approach some lady gynaecologists but, invariably, their team consisted of some men and they were not willing to make any adjustments. Neither was I.

The second condition was, of course, obvious – I would not give up my clay therapy. Not just that, I also insisted no medicine be administered to my baby and me. These conditions were, I am sure, rather drastic for some doctors. And many could not swallow the idea of being dictated by an apparent amateur. By this time I was into my seventh month and began to get a bit worried. And, almost as if by destiny, I suddenly met a wonderful, soft-spoken and highly qualified doctor. She was frank enough to admit she knew next to nothing about clay therapy but was, nevertheless, interested. She agreed to always consult me before she took any steps, and though she did prescribe routine medicines, I chose to avoid them.

There had been no untoward incidents during my pregnancy and I was certain I would have a normal delivery. I am glad Pascal prepared me for any emergency. But I was so sure was I about not having a Caesarian section that I never read up anything on the topic. I have a morbid fear of surgery. The sight of blood, no, even the thought of blood, is enough to make me feel faint!

As time went by and my due date approached, I felt a bit heavy with the weight of the baby. The baby was progressing well. I did not yet know its sex. We had decided there was no need to find out. All that we wanted was a healthy child.

On the morning of 14th September 2001 when I thought my pains were getting stronger, I went to the hospital. Initially, everything seemed fine. Then, during a routine check up, the doctor heard the child's heartbeat growing erratic. She discovered that the child had passed stool and was in danger of choking. I was, therefore, advised to undergo a Caesarean section as an emergency. The epidural was painful and I even had rigors. More than anything else, it was the shock of finding out that I would, after all, be operated upon.

The surgery was over in minutes. I was taken to a room and told that I had delivered a baby girl. I was certainly in pain. The doctor then came to give me an injection. I asked her what it was and she told me that it contained a mixture of antibiotics and painkillers. I reminded her about our deal. I would not take any medicine, I said. She insisted. Her biggest worry was infection. I reminded her that I would only continue with clay therapy. We got into an argument even as I kept insisting that the clay would take care of any setback. Pascal reiterated that clay was the best antiseptic. Finally, after a good deal of discussion, the doctor gave in and let me have my way. I applied clay over my stitches. When they were removed on the fifth day, I again put clay directly on the wound. Of course there was no infection! Within two months I went back to work. I had taken no painkillers, no antibiotics, no medicine of any sort after the surgery.

The baby weighed two and a half kilos at birth. She was neither vaccinated nor administered any medicines. Her eye sometimes watered and led to the formation of pus. We only applied clay as a preventive. When we became careless and stopped, her eye would again start to water from time to time till she was eight months old. I had gone to Australia for a conference and when I returned, I found that her eye infection was heavy. Worried, I put clay continuously for the next few days. In a week's time, the watering stopped and the infection cleared.

Tara has had her share of illnesses during the first year. Each time we only applied clay despite pressures from friends and well-wishers. Any big city has its share of environmental pollution, adulterated food, epidemics and a host of other problems. Tara's only option is to develop her immunity and I am convinced clay will help her on this journey.

IMPETIGO

As this book neared completion, Tara contracted an infectious skin disease. It started with an innocuous boil on her arm on which we put clay. Soon it started spreading into a larger area. Somehow, I did not take it seriously as I knew that clay helped pull out all sorts of infection. However, I have to admit I was lax about the applications. The infection got a grip of Tara and soon spread over her abdomen. Layers of skin peeled off and her flesh became exposed over many parts of her body. She looked torched. It resembled herpes and had us worried. That is when we started her clay applications in earnest. Later, we consulted medical books and came to the conclusion that is was impetigo, a disease that occurs in young children.

Clay applications were administered every three hours, including the nights. It took more than ten days for Tara's body to emerge victorious. It was a battle against an invisible invader. Our energies were taxed by comments from all and sundry who insisted we take her to the hospital. Tara was stoical throughout, though at times she cried when we removed the clay. It is important in skin diseases to wet the clay for easy removal. For this we sprinkled the area with natural spring water dipped in cotton wool. As we progressed, our baby would pull off the clay herself. Finally, Tara's wounds healed and she was cured. There are no scars. It was a long haul but we are confident of the knowledge that her body has developed its immunity because of clay.

MY EXPERIENCES WITH CLAY

Pascal Chazot

My mother, petite and originally partly Belgian, has a generous nature and a great sense of humour. But she also has a tremendous capacity to endure pain. Having borne six children, she continued to have a good deal of patience and unruffled pragmatism. My birth was dramatic and is still a great reminder to the family of her high tolerance levels. On 14th July, 1955, which is France's National Day, she was watching a programme when her labour pains started. Not wanting to miss out on the fun, she waited till the very end before going to the hospital. I was her fourth child, the quintessential prodigal!

I grew up in the north of France, in a small industrial town called Louvroil. Our house belonged to my maternal grandmother. By the time I was fifteen, I turned vegetarian. I used to also sit in *padmasana*, the lotus position that came naturally to me. Nepal became my new home when I was barely twenty. I went there to join my brother Eric and his wife Evelyne. My tryst with the Himalayan country turned into a more profound experience. I encountered a deeply spiritual yogi there, whom we called Dharma Guruju.

All this while I had been experimenting with different types of natural medicine, including Ayurvedic plants that the Himalayan region is so famous for. I had learnt Sanskrit at the Sorbonne University in Paris and studied the *Charakasamhita,* one of India's ancient texts on Ayurvedic medicine. This helped me make my own preparations. I had some knowledge about clay therapy and used it for minor cuts and bruises. Then, one day, when I burnt my hand, I applied clay and discovered its miraculous healing powers for blisters as well. Burns can be terribly agonizing but when I applied clay, the pain disappeared. This incident created, what is known in Neuro Linguistic Programming as, positive anchoring.

Once, when I had a mosquito bite on my leg, I applied clay on it. However, I left the bandage for nearly four days and let the clay dry. When

I finally took it off, it left a small mark on the skin, like a scar, and that took several months to disappear. Thus, while clay had cured the bite, it also left a blotch and I thought the process was not very successful. At that time I was not aware that one must not leave the application for too long. As a consequence, this minor incident retarded my use of clay as a complete cure.

In 1979, when I was staying near Kathmandu, I contracted an infection. It started rather inoffensively at the corner of my nostril. There was some discomfort but it did not appear to be dangerous. By evening, however, it started to rapidly travel upwards. An Ayurvedic doctor had given me some cream to apply. It may have been spoilt due to the container and only aggravated the situation. The infection spread and nearly reached my eye. It was a late winter evening and a weekend, so there was no question of seeking help. Thankfully, there was some clay in the house. Recalling its calming effect on minor injuries, I applied it during the night and nestled closer to the fire lit in the room. Every two hours I changed the application. I also tried to meditate and slept in fits and starts. Only when the clay dried would I wake up and apply a fresh coat. However, the first application itself put a brake on the galloping infection. By the third, the infection stabilized. Between the fourth and seventh, it began to reduce − rather slowly in the beginning but with great rapidity later. And after the eighth application, the infection had gone down to where it had started − at the corner of my nose.

I continued with the application the following night and was glad to note the infection had almost gone. In the morning, at around five., I was totally cured. With an incredible surge of energy I hurriedly packed a bag with some dry fruit and water, and set off on a trek towards the east. The next night I was in Tarke Gyang, having covered in one day a distance that normally takes three.

Since that decisive day, I have always sought the help of clay as the first resource whenever I have faced a health problem. In these past twenty-four years it has never let me down. More importantly, I have never needed any other medicines. It is certainly not mulish dogmatism that prevents my using anything else. It is just that I have never felt the need. Clay has sufficed as a complete, holistic cure.

GURUJU'S SCIATICA

During my stay in Kathmandu, spanning more than a decade, I was blessed to have encountered my guru who initiated me into Vajrayana Buddhism and forever changed my life. When I met him, he was nearly eighty years old. His wrinkled face sparkled with wisdom and humour, and he sported an active mind, with sharp mental faculties. A peaceful aura emanated from his humble yet beautiful dwelling, ensconced in the lap of the majestic Himalayas.

At eighty-five, he was just as active and even managed to dance in his magical garden. But one morning, suddenly overcome by acute pain in his right leg, he almost collapsed. A few days later he began to lose weight due to his immobility. His foot became dry and shrivelled. In the short span of a week local herbal medicines, allopathic drugs from a French doctor posted there, homeopathic pills from a native German doctor and even acupuncture were tried. However, none of these treatments had any effect. Guruju himself applied some oil and sun-bathed his leg in an attempt to get well. But day by day his condition worsened. Finally, with the help of X-rays, the French doctor diagnosed his problem as sciatica. The sciatic nerve had been severely pinched due to the erosion of the disc situated between the fourth and the fifth lumbar vertebrae.

Immediately, we resorted to Ayurveda, homeopathy and alternative therapies. The French doctor even prescribed allopathic medicines but was pessimistic due to Guruju's old age. The best professional healers from different systems and different countries, all known to our circle of friends, made sincere efforts. But to no avail.

Unable to remain a passive observer, I decided to intervene. I may have been a lay person in the field of medicine, but I was determined to use what had succeeded on me. I started applying red clay that was available and would regularly visit Guruju so that he applied clay two to three times. He used to sit out in the sun in his garden during the day and apply the clay himself once or twice at night.

In a short span of two days there was a radical change. Guruju's foot began to look healthy, though his ache had not receded. He remained enthusiastic the first three or four days. Thereafter, he felt the pain increasing. In fact, it seemed that the smarting would recede during the application but increase when the clay was removed. It took a while for us to realize this fact, after long discussions that went hand in hand with encouraging him to continue with the therapy. Five or six days later the pain diminished further. Then, after ten days, it reduced radically and within five weeks of the treatment he was fully cured. Never did the agony return and he lived till the age of ninety-seven.

LISSA'S TYPHOID

My daughter, Lissa, was eight years old when she got typhoid. She had a mosquito bite on her knee. It got infected. She put clay to heal it. Then she went to Nepal and I prepared to go abroad for a meeting. The day I was to leave, I got news that she had high fever and that her family had taken her for a blood test in order to diagnose her illness. I instructed them not to give her anything and wait for my arrival. I also told them to continue applying clay on her knee, as it could be the infection there that was bringing on the fever. I rushed and reached Nepal the following night.

The results of the test pointed to typhoid. However, the fever had already receded and was under control without any medication other than clay. I combined it with hipbaths in lukewarm water. The infection started to ooze out of the sore on her knee. In fact, the mouth of the wound increased and became large and deep. It was quite spectacular! I continued clay applications despite pressures. The next day her fever came down and in about four days' time she was back to normal. The inflammation on her knee took another week to heal. As a matter of fact, her typhoid was cured because of the clay applications for her knee, which became aggravated in the early stages in order to, ironically, allow rapid healing of a major disease.

FLU IN ALGERIA

During my stay in Algeria, where I was posted in 1988, a flu epidemic spread across Oran and I contracted the virus. Those afflicted suffered at least two weeks of raging fever. I met an acquaintance. He said that all those he knew, including himself, could do nothing but wait for this period in order to let the fever take its own course. Despite all kinds of medicines, allopathic and traditional, nothing helped. I, of course, suggested clay therapy, saying that this was what I would use if I fell ill. I even launched a verbal missile with much conviction and claimed that clay could cure the fever within forty-eight hours. But even as I said this, I was already feeling unwell. That very night I fell ill and had high fever with all the symptoms of the dreaded flu. I immediately started intensive, non-stop treatment with clay applications every two to three hours. In a span of thirty-six hours all the symptoms had disappeared. It took me just one more day of convalescence to be ready for work with renewed energy.

BELL'S PALSY

Returning from France and in transit in Delhi, I had to spend a night in a hotel near the airport. I contracted a very strange and unpleasant disease, probably by using the air-conditioning in the room. A few days later, while shaving in the morning, I realized that my face had gone numb. The muscles were paralysed! A pain developed in my jaw and during the course of the day spread to my teeth.

Under pressure from friends and colleagues (notably Anjou, to whom I was not married then and who was sceptical about clay therapy), I agreed to meet some specialists. I was told my condition was called Bell's Palsy and that it was a kind of viral attack. It could affect half my body. The eye too was in danger. The treatment proposed by the medical specialists consisted of a battery of medicines, both external – for application to the eyes – and internal. Also, painful electric shocks were recommended for my face. Coincidentally, I met a distant acquaintance just after my visit to this specialist. He apprised me of the absolute necessity of scrupulously following the treatment prescribed. He related to me that he had had the same affliction a year and a half ago and had gone to the doctor I had just visited. He said that he was, indeed, the best specialist in town. He revealed how happy he was to have followed the treatment, despite the painful shocks and the unpleasant side effects of the medicine. 'Thank God, I am out of it now…', he said and then, in a few moments added, 'Nearly out.' Then he smiled and revealed that half his mouth was still inert as a result of the paralysis. Watching his facial expression that resembled an ugly grimace, I resolved even more firmly to continue with the clay therapy. Thank heavens for my decision! Within fifteen days of intensive applications, I was well on my way to healing and in another week I was completely cured.

TYPES OF CLAY

There are several types of clay used across the world. The following are more commonly available:

1. Yellow clay or *multani mitti* (*gule-armani* in Gujarati and *gernumitti* in Hindi) is a variety of Bole Armeniac. This contains silicate of alumina, magnesia and iron oxide. The *Indian Materia Medica* reiterates that Bole Armeniac is refrigerant, astringent, absorbent and antiseptic.

Multani mitti has a yellowish appearance. It is found in the western part of India and the people of Multan, now in Pakistan, have known its use. It is said that women washed their hair and skin with this clay to retain their youthful looks. Today, this clay is still widely available for largely cosmetic purposes. It is mixed with face packs and also applied directly.

However, one needs to be wary of the quality that can differ from time to time. Sometimes, the clay has impurities and that can lessen its efficiency. We were once so happy with the healing powers of *multani mitti* that we purchased several kilos from the same shopkeeper on various occasions. Though he insisted it was from the same batch he had given us earlier, we discovered pieces of thread, sand, stone and even glass in the clay. Needless to say, such clay cannot and should not be used.

One disadvantage with *multani mitti* is that it takes a long time to soak up water and become a homogeneous paste. On an average it took the batch we had bought an average of twenty days to dissolve in water. So we had to be sure to soak the clay well in advance and keep watering it to keep it at the right consistency. In an emergency we had to resort to the French green clay that we had also kept at home.

2. *Gopichandan* (*shorakti* in Sanskrit and *pani-soka* in Hindi) is named after a lake near Dwarka in Gujarat called Gopi. It is found there in abundance. It is another variety of Bole Armeniac.

> It is a kind of clay – a magnesium iron and an aluminium yellow earth found in pieces of various shapes. Its smell resembles that of Multani Mati. . . . Water poured upon it is soon absorbed. It is used as an absorbent powder dusted on healthy ulcers and wounds. It is cooling and desiccant. It is applied with rose-water, as a paste, to the forehead to relieve headache, and also to inflamed boils.[11]

This clay is available in the form of small tablets. It took us a good amount of time to locate the source. We were always on the lookout for good local clay as it was not possible to always get clay from France. One day, in Ahmedabad, during an annual craft fair called 'Gurjari', organized by the government, we found some villagers selling white and yellow clay tablets. They were unable to explain its use, except for the fact that it could be used for washing one's face and hair. Later, we found that this clay is available in the local market and is called *gopichandan*. Mainly members of the Jain community apply it on the forehead during religious ceremonies.

However, this clay too was not consistent in its purity. As we required the clay in large quantities each time, we were often left with practically useless clay. So we continued our quest till we found the address of a villager from the city of Ambaji in Gujarat. Thereafter, we were assured of good quality clay and managed to stock up for emergencies.

3. *Geru* or red clay (*gairika* or *krishnamrittika* in Sanskrit; China clay kaolinite, kaolin, porcelain clay and red ochre in English; *girimati* in Bengali and *chiknimati* or *geru* in Hindi) is a native white aluminium silicate and iron oxide found mainly in Sri Lanka and China. It is obtained by purifying native white fulspar or aluminium silicate by elutriation, which removes silica and under-composed fulspar. Thus it can be converted into a soft, whitish and earthy mass. It can also be pulverized but remains insoluble in water or in dilute acids'.[12]

The *Indian Materia Medica* defines one of the qualities of this
clay as relieving bleeding from internal organs. It is used in the preparation
of Ayurvedic medicines.

There are 2 varieties: bole (yellow) and red ochre. The red
ochre contains more iron than the bole and is used in
medicine. It sometimes occurs in powder form and sometimes as hard pieces; "'Gairika': hematite, which is red and
often hard, and limonite which is yellow or brown, both
occur in the form of ochres." – Sir P. C. Ray. It rapidly
absorbs water if poured upon it. It is purified by being
soaked in milk seven times and is sweetish, astringent,
cooling, useful as a local application to burns, ulcers, boils,
pustular eruptions and aphthous sores about the mouth. It
is rarely used internally except as an ingredient of some
compound preparations containing a large number of
mineral drugs, for instance Jvara-kunjara Paridra Rasa
which contains nearly all the mineral substances. Besides
gairika several other varieties of earth are occasionally used
in medicine; e.g. a sweet scented earth brought from Surat
and called Saurashtra Mrittika is astringent and useful in
haemorrhages. It enters into the composition of several
medicines for relieving bleeding from internal organs.

In powder form, *geru* is often used for painting walls and pots
because of its red colour. Gandhiji writes that he used red earth which,
when combined with water, would emit a sweet, delicate smell.

4. Black clay is found in some villages in Gujarat and its
neighbouring states. We did manage to procure it with difficulty. However,
we were not really satisfied with it and discontinued using it.

5. Green clay is purified clay, green in colour as the name
suggests. We purchase our stock from France. Easily available in medical
shops, in French it is called *argile verte concassée*. Best purchased in lots
of three kilos, it is available in both large and small pieces. If you wish to
purchase it in powder form, it becomes more expensive. We suggest you
buy the standard three-kilogram packets. Green clay can be applied even
on open wounds.

6. White clay is also available in France but is mainly efficient for face packs and cosmetic purposes. Moreover, it is available only in small packs and is expensive. It appears to be less efficient than the green clay we have been using regularly.

7. Calcium montmorillonite clay or *the living clay* is an age-old substance of nature. Only a limited number of calcium montmorillonite clay deposits remain around the world. The name montmorillonite comes from Montmorillon in France where this clay was initially discovered in the 1800s. Dr. Simon Cohen states:

> A recognized detoxifying agent, nutrient and bactericidal 'Calcium Montmorillonite Clay' is in the smectite group of clays. Only those clays within the smectite group have the ability to absorb. Its power as a detoxifying substance comes from its inherent ability to adsorb and absorb. Its unique ability to grow and change (adsorb) is the reason for its classification and recognition as a 'Living Clay'. While there is more than one Montmorillonite, the red 'Calcium Montmorillonite Clay' of the smectite group remains a favorite for human use.[13]

Sodium montmorillonite, the other variety of Montmorillonite, is commonly known as bentonite. This is principally used for industrial purposes.

8. Terramin is another type of montmorillonite clay that is edible, can be easily ingested and, hence, is the preferred choice by many for themselves and for animals and plants as well.

Gandhiji wrote that it was safe to use soft alluvial clay that is neither gritty nor sticky. However, one should not take clay from soil that contains manure.

Every region will have its own source of good clay but the problem is to locate it. The quest for good quality clay is already part of the struggle to keep good health. And this is certainly not easy. If there is no clay available in the market, one can try the countryside. Try to get clay deep down from the underground either by digging or from a place that has been already dug up. The location must be away from all sources of pollution. One must dig up to a metre deep in order to obtain pure clay.

If the clay appears to be pure, try applying it on the hand and watch for any reaction. You will come to know by its feel and aspect whether it is suitable for use. Impurities can be detected visually or by the way it reacts. Don't use clay that has been sullied by sand. Pure clay, when dissolved in water, must appear smooth and homogeneous in all aspects. A small spoonful of clay can be dissolved in a glass of water. Impurities, if any, will rise to the surface.

If you have the time and the resources:

Dissolve the clay in a lot of water first.

Sieve the clay several times to remove impurities. Use a fine sieve or a coarse piece of cloth for this purpose.

Dry the clay in the sun. Allow the water to evaporate. This may take several days. Thereafter, take the clay and store it in an earthen jar.

If the clay you obtain is reasonably pure, you can apply it on any part of the body. Take care, however, not to use it on your eyes or any other cavity or orifice, unless you are absolutely sure of its quality. We only use green clay from France for open wounds, our eyes and, for healing, even eat it.

METHOD OF PREPARING CLAY FOR USE

Materials required:
Earthen vessel
Clay
Water
Wooden spoon/spatula
Cloth

Clay must be put in an earthen jar and soaked in water that is as pure and natural as possible. Tap water is preferable to water that has undergone filtration with the UV (ultra violet ray) technology. Even though tap water may be treated with chemicals, it still retains some minerals. Water that is filtered through the UV technology is safe for drinking but is dead water. Therefore, it should not be used for preparing clay for therapy.

Put enough water to cover the clay. In a while, it would have absorbed the water and look like a homogeneous paste. If it is very runny, then add some more clay and wait. If too dry, then add just enough water to give the clay its right consistency for use.

Stir to dissolve lumps with a wooden or porcelain spoon or spatula. Under any circumstances, do not use metal. This oxidizes the clay and makes it lose much of its properties. Avoid a plastic spoon as well.

Allow the clay to stand for an hour. Sometimes, clay can be ready in as short a while as thirty minutes. But it is preferable to allow it to stand for a longer time. The clay is ready when it has absorbed all the water and there are no hard lumps. It should not be so liquid that it runs when you apply it on cloth strips. Nor should it be so dry that it appears unduly hard.

Note:

If you are using the white clay, it will be ready fairly quickly, within thirty minutes. It needs less water compared to the green clay.

Green clay takes even lesser time to be ready for use – about fifteen minutes. However, it needs a little more water, as it is denser in consistency.

Multani mitti or yellow clay needs more time – several days to dissolve completely.

METHOD OF APPLICATION
AND USE

EXTERNAL USE

Quantity to be used per application

The quantity to be applied must be a handful of wet clay paste. This quantity is to be maintained for all ailments and irrespective of where it is being applied for all external applications. Put the clay in a thick, two-inch layer on a strip of cloth before tying it on the affected area.

A very thin layer can be good for the skin but cannot heal, and remains superficial. The clay must be in contact with your skin. Keep the application on for at least two to three hours till it dries and peels off easily. In case the clay turns dry and hardens, soften it with water before peeling it off gently.

Ideally, clay must be moist when it is removed so that it leaves no traces on the body. If removed too early, it remains sticky and parts of it cling to the skin. Over a period of time, your body will tell you when the cloth needs to be removed. This can happen even when you sleep. You will wake up, as the application will suddenly feel heavy, dry or itchy. Sometimes, with just a single application, you could sleep through the night without any discomfort. In any case, trust the clay and your body.

Throw away the clay that has been used and never ever reuse it. It is full of toxins. Clay can be reused only when it is scrupulously dissolved in water, dried again and re-purified. Gandhiji wrote that unclean clay should be dried, pounded and passed through a fine sieve. It can be also heated and thus sterilized. He often reused the same clay for treatment after drying it in the sun, pounding it and painstakingly sieving it.

If you have the time and sufficient infrastructure, go ahead and decontaminate clay that has been used, and reuse it.

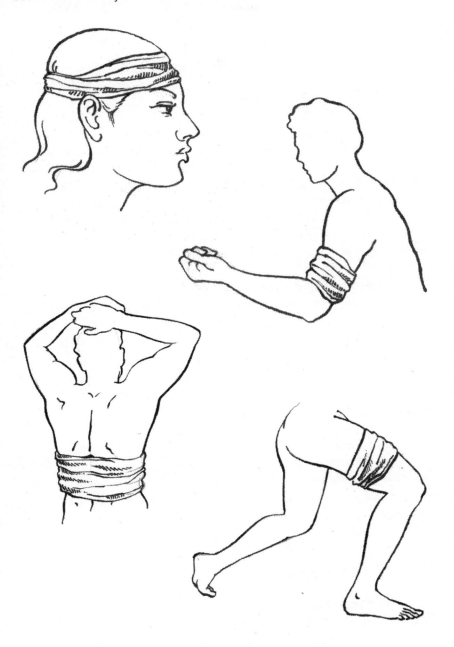

We have never really purified clay. In fact, as a symbolic gesture, we have made a conscious effort to throw it away, absolutely aware that we are actually also throwing away the disease and getting rid of our ailments forever. Specialists often dwell on the psychosomatic nature of various actions. We find this act thoroughly cleansing. By externalizing an internal ailment, we translate it into dynamic action.

Application on the eyes

If you need to use clay on your eyes but feel queasy, apply it on a gauze bandage and then put it across your lids. This will protect the eyes from irritation, in case the clay is not pure, and prevent it from direct contact. However, pure clay can be applied straight on the eyes and brings immediate relief. It also soothes tiredness helps remove infections. However, if it happens to sting and feels uncomfortable, wash it off and try applying it elsewhere close to the eye area such as your forehead. Remember to place a handful of clay on the strip of cloth before placing it over the eyes and tying up the cloth around the head.

Open cuts and wounds

If there is an open wound, apply clay that is pure or sterilized. Do not worry about it penetrating the injury. It will only give it a good coating and help heal. When you remove the clay, there is no need to wash off what is stuck on the wound. You can simply put a fresh application over the bits and pieces that have not come off. The clay will absorb all the infection. Once again, a good amount (at least a handful of wet clay) must be applied for it to be effective.

Genital area

In minor irritations, wash the area several times with water that has been diluted with clay. In more extreme cases, wet clay can be directly inserted and the external area washed. If the clay dries and creates discomfort, simply wash the area clean.

INTERNAL USE

Drinking clay

In case of indigestion, gastroenteritis, ulcers or other intestinal ailments, you can even drink clay. For this, dissolve a tablespoon into a porcelain or wooden glass with a non-metalic spoon. Use a wooden stick or spoon. Normally, the clay will settle at the bottom while the water will get charged with all the minerals. Leave it overnight and sip it on an empty stomach early next morning. There is no need to stir the settled clay before drinking. If it is an emergency and you cannot wait, let the clay dissolve sufficiently before drinking it. Thereafter, add a teaspoon of clay to recharge the water and wait a while before the second dose.

Do not drink clay for more than ten days. In some cases it can lead to constipation. If that persists, give yourself a break and apply the clay externally. You can restart drinking clay a few days later, if you so desire.

The *Indian Materia Medica* gives examples of the internal use of red ochre clay, mainly in cases of dysentery.

Eating clay
Clay can be eaten as well. In cases of toothache, for example, a piece of clay can be kept in the mouth and allowed to slowly dissolve. This can be done as often as it is comfortable. Again, it is better to give a small break after ten days and restart the treatment a few days later. Eating clay soothes chronic ulcers and other stomach ailments. Its powers of absorption ensure that all acidity disappears in a matter of a few minutes. It also recharges the body with necessary minerals.

Eating clay too often may lead to minor constipation. Therefore it is advisable to always give a gap of fifteen to twenty days after eating or drinking clay for a week.

For enema
Purified clay can be dissolved in water and used for the purpose of cleaning the intestines. For an enema, use just a spoonful. This not only cleans, but also drains out the toxins and heals any intestinal disorders. Using clay in an enema is extremely beneficial and efficient.

USING CLAY

Using clay is absolutely safe. Only take care to use clay that is pure, both externally and for ingesting it. Clay applications do lead to some fatigue and a desire to sleep. Follow your body's advice as this is nature's way of rejuvenation. It is probably because the clay acts on our metabolism and stimulates the body's reserves to act on an ailment. Many first-time users panic and complain that the use of clay makes them feel weak and lethargic. The accompanying fatigue is a normal reaction, especially when clay is used intensively. If the ailment is not too severe or the treatment really urgent, use clay only at night before going to sleep.

Clay galvanizes the body into action by tapping its internal resources of energy and healing powers. Once you start to use it, be sure to continue till you are cured. Never start using clay if you are not sure of continuing. First-time users feel that as the substance has no side effects (apart from curing other illnesses), it can be employed intermittently. This is a complete misconception. Gentle as this medicine is, it is also very potent and powerful. Therefore, do not play around by just trying it now and then, or in combination with other chemical-based allopathic drugs. Start when you are thoroughly convinced and sure to persist with the treatment.

Sometimes, the ailment may appear to get worse before actually diminishing and then getting absolutely cured. This is because clay absorbs all the toxins from the body and the process takes time. You must simply continue with the application. An open wound may even become large, with pus and infection. Do not panic. The wound will heal when the body is restored to health. The curative properties of clay ensure that the skin becomes better and scars, if any, lighter. They may even disappear altogether.

There is a great deal of experimentation and trial and error in the use of clay. Much depends upon the quality of its purity. In some cases, there can be a reaction on the area of application in the form of small boils, pimples or rashes. This is quite rare but if it occurs there is no reason to be frightened. Actually, it is a good sign – it signifies that the body is actually reacting and eliminating the toxins! Be consistent and continue applying the clay on the same spot till the body rids itself of the infection altogether. We know of cases where an application enlarged a small boil into such a large and deep wound that it appeared as if the clay was performing a surgery! After a few days, when the infection poured out in the form of pus and blood, the wound healed without any trace of a scar.

Sometimes, the treatment may make you feel uncomfortable. There could be some irritation on the area where you have applied the clay. If this happens, remove it and re-apply on another part. If the irritation persists, then chances are that the clay may not be of good quality and it is better to purchase another batch.

MAJOR REACTIONS FROM SOCIETY

If you are using clay, be prepared for major reactions and outbursts from your family and friends. The response may range from scepticism to tirades on the dangers of taking your health into your hands.

For some strange and unexplained reason herbal concoctions and aromatherapy find better acceptance. But using clay appears to be too radical in its simplicity. Facing such diverse reactions is very difficult. There is constant pressure that we must first diagnose the disease. For clay users, giving a name to the disease is unimportant, as the cure remains the same – treatment by clay. Then there is the perception that one is taking unnecessary risks, that clay is all right for minor diseases but it cannot cure everything. If one chooses to apply clay as a complete therapy on one's child, you may even end up being called mad!

Societal influences can be unrelenting and the pressures may be so well mounted that you may start to vacillate. In fact, research conducted by psychiatrists R. D. Laing and A. Esterson has shown how major psychotic diseases may be or are the result and even the symptom of societal pressures, especially those put by the family.[14] They go to the extent of saying that it is the environment that is schizophrenic and not the individual.

Both individuals and structures exploit the many insecurities related to ignorance of one's own health, the fears of ill health and, of course, death. The exploitation may be largely due to economic interests. But also well-intentioned family members and friends can, in their zeal to help, do more damage than good. This is exemplified well in the famous film *One Flew Over the Cuckoo's Nest.*

Clay appears to be an absurdly simple remedy. In an era of super specialization, the doubt often raised by sceptics is whether there can be one cure for all human beings and all diseases. Organized structures rule our lives. Health is a large industry, involving incredibly large sums of money. Therefore, the practice of clay shakes the very foundations of such an industry. At the micro level, it shakes the certitude of individuals who have become completely dependent for the smallest things in life. Therefore, can one really be free in the domain of something as important as health? In a consumerist society, where major health structures are money spin-offs, can there be a remedy as cheap as clay?

EVEN ANIMALS USE CLAY!

Animals are great users of clay. Some are known to eat clay while others roll in it for finding a cure. Elephants constantly sprinkle earth on their bodies. Tigers eat clay to cure stomach ailments. Deer use it to heal open wounds. Certainly, the animal kingdom has an innate sense of curing themselves with the help of this wonderful therapy. When applying clay on your pets, remember to tie the bandage securely. When you are removing it, use water to first dilute the dry clay or else it will pull off the coat and cause unnecessary pain.

We have applied clay cataplasms to ailing cats, dogs and even our horse that had a leg injury. It required very large bandages and huge amounts of clay. But he was cured with just a few applications.

A FACE PACK FOR THE TAJ MAHAL!

According to newspaper reports, the archaeological department, to give the Taj Mahal a facelift, is now using the common *multani mitti*, favoured by women in face packs. It will be applied to scrub off the dirt and remove blemishes caused by pollution.

AND NOW, A CLAY T-SHIRT!

Wearing a clay t-shirt cures asthma. According to research in the U.S.A. clay t-shirts also emit Far Infra-Red Rays (FIR) and keep diseases away from astronauts when they are denied the health-inducing merits of sunlight. Shirts, knee caps, gloves and even undergarments made of a special clay mined out of the sea bed act as supplementary medicine. Interestingly, this study was reportedly initiated after it was discovered that Asians, who traditionally used earthen pots for cooking, were blessed with longer life span. Thus, sand found in the ocean bed was treated by heating to develop the product that went into the making of these t-shirts.

This special bio-ceramic clay is developed by a Malaysian organization with Korean technology. Bio-ceramic t-shirts alleviate pain from serious injuries, as well as help relieve aching knees damaged by osteo-arthritis. They are also known to be beneficial for hypertension. Now bio-ceramic bands and braces are available according to newspaper reports. The latest is a bio-ceramic pillow that helps asthma patients.[15]

CLAY AS A THERAPY FOR CHILDREN

Clay is used as therapy for disturbed children. Those who are visually impaired can also use it successfully. Children are encouraged to actively manipulate the clay, at times even with aggression. Hostility and violence, otherwise a taboo, gets a release when children come into contact with clay.

Clay is malleable, has weight and texture, and a smell that children often love. It responds to them by changing its form, engaging them in a sort of tactile conversation. Diluting it can alter its consistency. Drying or firing it can modify its form. Thus, manipulating clay helps a child develop fine motor skills and is often used in pre-school classes.

Apart from releasing negative energy, clay also allows the child an extensive opportunity for creativity and has come to be used for varied activities like play, art, physiotherapy, relaxation and the development of speech and cognitive skills. Finally, clay is non-toxic, eco-friendly and easily available. It is an excellent toy for children and a creative medium for adults, apart, of course, from its great therapeutic qualities.

WHEN CLAY DOES NOT WORK

Sometimes clay does not seem to work or has a slow effect. This may be due to a disease that is deeply ingrained or because of improper use. Perhaps the clay was too dry or removed too early. Or, the applications may have been too few and far between. If clay does not work, it may be because of some impurity. Dissolve a portion in water to see whether this is true. Sometimes, certain types of clay are less efficient than others. Procure it from another source. Also, the brand can make a difference. We once purchased a good amount of green clay in France from a particular company. Upon using it, we felt that it was slower in its efficiency. Then we discovered pieces of stone and rock in the packets. So we switched to another company, Argiletz, and have been very satisfied. In India, we sometimes found bits and pieces of stone, thread and glass in the yellow clay we were using. Needless to say, we threw out the entire lot. Our quest continued till we located a source near the village of Ambaji in Gujarat. Certainly, the search for good quality clay is in itself a struggle. But it is also part of the whole process of healing!

SOME COMMON AILMENTS

The frequency of the applications will depend on the intensity of the pain or the gravity of the ailment. The more acute the condition, the more intensive the treatment. But a minimum of two to three applications is a prerequisite for any complaint. If the illness is serious or life threatening, then we suggest continuous applications till the problem is eased.

Acidity
Clay is very effective in cases of acidity, as it has great powers of absorption. Drink a spoonful of clay dissolved in water once a day on an empty stomach. Continue for a week. You can also suck on a piece of clay and allow it to slowly dissolve in the mouth whenever acidity occurs.

Acne
For acne or pimples, apply a thick layer of clay on the affected area. Cover with a wet cloth for at least an hour. As this may mean resting while the application is on, you could also put a clay cataplasm on the upper arm. This will regulate the hormonal imbalances and remove toxins. Continue to wash you face with a clay paste rather than soap.

Anaemia
Dissolve a spoonful of clay in a glass of water. Allow it to stand overnight and drink it in the morning. Continue for a week and resume after a gap of fifteen to twenty days.

Appendicitis
Apply clay cataplasms on the lower part of the abdomen and continue for a few days even after the pain subsides.

Arthritis
Apply clay cataplasms on the knees or the joints where there is pain. Try at least one application in the morning and one at night, before

going to sleep. If you do not get up at night, it is all right to keep the clay on till the morning. Continue these applications for at least a month in case you are not fully cured. Sometimes the process may take longer.

Asthma

Drink a spoonful of clay dissolved in water once a day for ten days. Then resume after a gap of another ten days. Try this for a month. Combine this treatment with clay applications on the upper arm at least once a day and once a night, and continue till you feel better.

Bells Palsy

Apply clay cataplasms intensively on that part of face where there is no sensation. Continue till complete recovery is made and even after.

Blood pressure

For both high and low blood pressure, apply clay cataplasms on the upper arm at least once a day and once at night. Continue for a few extra days after the blood pressure returns to normal.

Burns

Clay is miraculous when it comes to healing burns. Purified clay must be applied immediately onto the injury. Continuously change the applications till the pain is reduced and new skin starts to appear. Do not worry if the skin peels or if there is some pus formation. By and by, clay will absorb all the infection if it is pure. Impurities, however, will irritate the skin. And if this happens, immediately remove the application.

Once the pain has gone and the wound has begun to heal, you may also sprinkle clay, pulverized into fine powder, directly on the lesion. A wet application, however, is most efficient. It is also a great pain reliever and absorbs the heat from the burn. This is because of the wet clay that has a cooling effect and provides that much needed respite. Even in cases of third degree burns, try covering the area with purified clay cataplasms.

Cancer

Start by applying clay cataplasms on the upper arm. Continue for a few days and observe the consequences. If there is any reaction in the form of boils, pimples or rashes, it is a good sign. Continue applying clay on the same spot as the body has found an outlet. If there is no reaction whatsoever, then apply clay on the affected part where there is a cancerous growth. It is important to mention that several cases of cancer have been completely cured by using clay. The patient must, however, continue diligently with the therapy for a long time and not succumb to using a combination of allopathic drugs and other alternative remedies. They may combine the use of clay with a proper diet that must, essentially, comprise vegetable juices and eat frugally. In fact, it is best to literally starve the cancerous cells that feed on a rich diet.

Colitis

As for all problems located in a sensitive area, start by applying clay cataplasms on the upper arm. Continue for two or three days. Then apply clay cataplasms on the stomach, at the level of the big intestine, where the pain is the most acute. Continue for several weeks. In addition to this, drink purified clay for a period of ten days. Resume drinking after giving a gap of eight to ten days each time.

Coma

Apply clay cataplasm on the forehead, continuously changing it every two hours.

Common cold

Apply cataplasms of clay on the forehead or the neck. For quickest results, apply clay on the nose. This, however, could be uncomfortable because you may have to secure the clay with a bandage and breathe from the mouth. Otherwise, apply the treatment on one side of the nose so that you can breathe with the help of the other free nostril.

Conjunctivitis

Apply clay cataplasms on the forehead or in extreme cases on the eyes after placing a gauze over the eyes to protect them from irritation. Clay cataplasms can be put on the upper arm in cases of discomfort and to divert the toxins to another place. Putting the clay on the eyes directly can initially worsen or prolong the ailment as the clay will draw the toxins from that particular place. In one case within twenty-four hours of applying clay only on the upper arm, despite the patient's scepticism, chronic conjunctivitis was cured. The patient had been suffering for several years.

Constipation

Constipation can be cured by overnight applications of clay poultices on the stomach. Continue for a few nights and resume after a gap of fifteen to twenty days. Clay can also be eaten or dissolved in a glass of water and drunk the next morning.

Gandhiji used mud poultices on his stomach and writes about its efficacy. He mentions Just's written treatise where it is mentioned that clay can be eaten to overcome constipation. Gandhiji never ate clay though he recommended that it be tried. In our experience, we have on several occasions eaten purified clay and can vouch for its benefits.

In cases of extreme and chronic constipation, clay applications can be combined with an enema at least once in two to three days, for a period of ten days.

Eczema

Apply clay cataplasm on that part of the body where you experience the dry and itchy feeling. It is possible that boils may appear or even some rashes. This is a normal reaction. Just continue applying clay till skin is healed.

Diarrhoea

Dissolve a spoonful of clay in a glass of water and let it stand for a while. Drink the water two to three times a day. Also apply clay on the stomach, especially over the area where the intestines lie. If you get diarrhoea while you are working or travelling, then suck on a dry piece of clay from time to time for relief.

Diabetes

Start by applying clay on the upper arm. It is important to continue with clay applications regularly. Apart from applications at night, try and put clay poultices during the daytime as well. After a month, the night application can be put over the area where the pancreas lies to directly stimulate the organ. During the day, the application can be put on the arm as usual.

Dysentery

Dissolve a spoonful of clay in water at night and drink it on an empty stomach in the morning. Combine this with clay applications on the stomach. In case of acute dysentery, drink clay twice a day and intensively apply clay externally till you are totally cured.

Eyesight

For poor eyesight apply clay on the back of the neck. This acts on the optic nerves. If it is not possible to apply clay during the day, then apply at least once in the evening and, later, once at night. It is a good idea to also combine this treatment with eye exercises that will strengthen the weak muscles.

Aldous Huxley, the famous writer, became a victim of failing eyesight. He cured himself with clay applications and went on to continue with his writings.

Fever

Apply cataplasms of clay on the forehead as it provides great relief in high temperatures. Change the application as soon as it feels hot or dry. If the temperature continues to soar, try hipbaths.

Gangrene

Apply clay cataplasms intensively on the infection. Also drink clay mixed in water. According to one patient, the infection initially appeared to spread before decreasing and healing. It appears that there are cases where a gangrene infection was totally healed within eight months.

Gastroenteritis

Dissolve a spoonful of clay in a glass of water and let it stand for sometime. Drink the water two to three times a day. Also continue with clay applications on the stomach. From time to time suck on a dry piece of clay if you are working or travelling.

Haemorrhage

Immediately put external applications on the affected area. If that is not possible then put it as close to the haemorrhage as you can.

Hysteria

In cases of hysteria, not only the epigastric pulsations become reduced but also the intensity of other disturbances of the abdominal organs, with the disappearance of the

58

vomiting, diarrhoea and abdominal pains, became notably reduced. In Wologda (Russia) women soothe the pains of hysteria by applying clay to the soles of the feet.

Dr. Loueacheveitch reports several cases of gonorrhoeal epididymitis promptly cured by the application of white moulding clay of sculptors made into a paste with water. The dressings are removed twice a day; the swellings are said to subside on the 2nd or 3rd day.[16]

Infertility

Apply clay cataplasms on your lower stomach. Continue for several weeks, or even several months. Combine this with internal use. Drink a spoonful of clay that has been dissolved in water and kept overnight. Drink it on an empty stomach once a day for a period of ten days. Then give a gap of twenty to twenty-five days before resuming the treatment.

Insomnia

Apply clay cataplasms on the forehead before sleeping. If there is no effect after three or four days, try applying clay over the area where the liver lies and observe any changes. Clay helps detoxify the liver and provides relief.

Malaria

Clay can be applied on the forehead as malaria brings on high fever. Continue successive applications on the forehead till the fever abates.

Migraine

Apply cataplasms of clay on the forehead or on the upper part of the neck, over the medulla oblangata. If there is no relief, apply it over the area that houses our liver. You could also apply clay on the stomach as gastric problems often bring on attacks of migraines.

Acupressure on points such as the temples, behind the ears, around the nose and even on the hands provides relief. For this, consult the acupressure charts.

Menstruation cramps

Apply clay cataplasms on the lower abdomen or below the stomach. Two to three applications may be enough to provide relief.

However, continue till you are cured of this common ailment that afflicts so many girls and young women.

Obesity
Clay cataplasms can be applied on the upper arm. If the patient suffers from any gland problem that is the cause of obesity, treatment can be continued in a similar manner but with external applications relocated to the glandular area as well.

Paralysis
Apply clay cataplasms on that part of the body that is severely paralysed. Try to cover as much as possible of the affected part. The cure may take a long time and you have to be very patient for benefits to show.

Rheumatism
Clay is used extensively in health centres in France for this malady. Patients are even immersed in tubs of clay as part of the healing process. Intensive clay applications on painful areas of the body are effective.

Sciatica
Put cataplasms on the lower back for immediate relief from the pain. During the day, clay applications can be continued on the arm unless the ache is severe. If this happens, continue applications on the lower back, accompanied by complete bed rest.

Sores, cuts and wounds
Apply clay directly on the wound or on the infected area. If clay enters the wound do not bother washing it off. Simply continue to put fresh applications. Remember to use only purified clay; otherwise the wound can become infected. The injury may appear to worsen, with pus and swelling as the clay gets to draw out the toxins, but there is no need to worry. As long as the clay is pure, there is no danger. Continue with the treatment till you are cured.

Throat infection, cough, tonsilitis
Apply clay cataplasms on the throat for immediate results. As it is applied directly, the infection or cough may initially worsen. If you are uncomfortable, the cataplasm can be put on the forehead or upper arm.

60 This will divert the infection though relief may also be proportionally less. Suck on a piece of clay for an aching throat.

Thyroid

Start by clay applications on the upper arm. If no reactions appear in the form of rashes or boils, then apply clay on the affected glandular area.

Toothache

For aching and swollen gums or a toothache, tuck a small piece of clay in the mouth, on or close to the infected area, and allow it to dissolve. There is no harm if the clay enters the body. It is easier to put clay in the mouth at night and sleep. In the morning, spit out the clay that has not dissolved. For a serious infection, put clay application on the outer cheek at least twice a day for several days. This will hasten your recovery.

Ulcers

When eaten, clay provides great relief to people suffering from ulcers. As clay has great properties of absorption, it lines the stomach walls and absorbs all the acidity that causes the pain. For ulcers, a longer treatment is recommended, along with external applications.

Urinary tract infection

Put clay cataplasms on your lower stomach. This may be a little cumbersome. Try securing the clay tightly with a stretch band. A little clay can also be inserted into the orifice to absorb infection and reduce swelling. It will be expelled when you pass urine. Continue intensively for a few days after you are cured so that the infection does not recur.

Viral fever

Apply clay cataplasms on the forehead intensively till the fever is under control. Then you can shift the application to the upper arm till complete recovery is made. Combine clay treatment with hipbaths to bring down the high fever.

Yeast and fungal infection

Apply clay cataplasms on or near the affected part. Continue with at least two to three applications per day.

THE ECONOMICS OF CLAY

What Gandhiji wrote about the exorbitant fees charged by doctors is true even today. Moreover, add the cost of medicines and any prolonged treatment can turn out to be prohibitively expensive. People are known to fall to ruin because of this.

Let us consider the economics of clay:
- Clay is cheap. It is affordable even to those in a low income group.
- It has a lifelong shelf life! Dry clay can be kept for as long as you want. It cannot get spoilt. If it is wet, it will become naturally dry and remain in the vessel. As long as it is protected from outside dust and impurities, clay can be stocked and used any time.
- It is economical in terms of infrastructure. All that is required is a vessel, water, wooden spatula and some cloth. Sometimes, perhaps, you may need the help of another person to tie the bandage of cloth. Your bedside table or a corner in your room is enough to create your healing counter.
- The side effects of using clay are only positive! If you use clay for any one problem, it will act on the rest of your body and cure other ailments as well. This is in complete opposition to some forms of chemical drugs that supposedly act on one ailment but create enough dangerous side effects that need to be treated as well. In many cases, if the treatment you undergo does not cure you, you could return with just the side effects that become a handicap for life.
- It acts on the whole organism and goes to where the infection is imbedded. This means that there is no need to undergo expensive and sometimes painful tests to know what the ailment is. Clay is an active and intelligent agent that touches the root malady and galvanizes the body into making its own antibodies to combat the disease.

- It is economical in terms of energy. In naturopathy you do not suppress the ailment. You take it positively and act upon it. Clay helps the body mobilize its own resources to fight the ailment. This means that there is little likelihood of the same ailment becoming a recurrent feature. Therefore, in future your energy will not be wasted for the same purpose.
- Rather than weaken the body, clay fortifies it with each successive application.
- Whatever the diagnosis, the treatment with clay is the same. So no harm is done. Practitioners of clay therapy are not anxious to know the name of the disease as the cure is the same.

In its issue of February 1926 the *Indian Medical Gazette* states that after the astonishing results of the use of kaolin for the treatment of cholera by Dr. Kuhne the advantages are obvious.

- It can be administered by anyone, even by the patient herself.
- Accurate dosage is not necessary.
- In an hour, a hundred patients can be treated.
- The treatment is not painful.
- It is free from danger.
- It requires no special appliances.
- It can be used as a prophylactic measure.
- It is very cheap.

THE PROPERTIES OF CLAY

Clay can absorb

Clay has excellent powers of absorption. It has thus the capacity to attract and absorb the toxins in the body. According to the *Indian Materia Medica*, "Kaolin (or clay) probably owes its value to (a) absorption on the surface of its fine molecules of toxins; thus, it is of great value in cases of food poisoning also".[17]

Clay has minerals

In an increasingly urbanised world, our body is constantly attacked by pollution in the air, water and even in the pesticide-ridden food we consume. The filtered and boiled water that we drink is often dead, as it does not contain any minerals. Vegetables that are grown in reused soil with artificial fertilizers lose essential minerals that are required by our body. Applications of clay, both external and internal, refurbish the body of the deficient minerals and help attain its normal balance.

Dextreit writes that clay contains oxides, bioxydes, trioxydes etc with the following composition as per detailed scientific analysis:[18]

Silica:	31.14 to 41.38 %
Titane:	0.47 to 1.89 %
Aluminium:	40.27 to 48.13 %
Iron:	0.11 to 0.78 %
Calcium:	0.05 to 0.13 %
Magnesium:	traces upto 0.05 %
Sodium and potassium:	0.25 to 0.85 %

The Pure Kaolin analysed in the *Indian Materia Medica* has been found to contain:[19]

Alumina:	70 %
Silica:	26 %
Iron oxide:	4 %

This analysis is, however, not sufficient to explain the wonderful healing properties of clay. Calcium montmorillonite, the second type of montmorillonite, is also known as *living clay*. It principally consists of minerals that enhance the production of enzymes in all living organisms.

Clay replenishes minerals in our body
It is clear that clay contains important minerals such as calcium, iron, magnesium, potassium, manganese, and silica, as well as traces of other elements. The body needs minerals in order to remain healthy. Moreover, it needs a source of replenishment as it is not equipped to produce minerals.

"The body can tolerate a deficiency of vitamins for a longer period of time than it can a deficiency of minerals. A slight change in the blood concentration of important minerals may rapidly endanger life," says F. P. Anita, M. D., in his book *Clinical Dietetics and Nutrition* (1989).

The fact that different minerals exist in a natural proportion makes clay a substance that is easily absorbed by the body.

A website on clay therapy informs us of the following:

Minerals perform a number of important functions. They:
1. Supply major elements and trace elements that may be lacking in the diet.
2. Act as catalysts, thus playing a major role in metabolism and cell building.
3. Regulate the permeability of cell membranes.
4. Maintain water balance and osmotic pressure between the inside and outside environment.
5. Influence the contractility of muscles.
6. Regulate the response of nerves to stimuli.

Why are minerals so important to the chemical reactions in the human body? The cell is like an electrical battery, with positive and negative charges. When the energy of the battery begins to weaken, the cell becomes sick and weak. However, if the dying cell is charged by an

electrical current it will once again become living.
Minerals themselves hold positive and electrical charges.
The exchange of these charges accounts for its action.
Scientists are not sure exactly how this works or to what
degree it does. Yet, when the cell is given the essential
minerals it needs to live, it can regenerate and 'nurse'
itself back to health.

Calcium Montmorillonite Clay is reported to contain no
less than 67 minerals. This impressive assortment of
minerals includes calcium, iron, magnesium, potassium,
manganese, and silica, as well as trace elements,
appearing in very tiny amounts. The mineral content
being extremely high sets the stage for replenishing
dietary deficiencies. Today, more than ever, diets are
lacking essential trace minerals and micronutrients.
Without basic minerals, life cannot exist; without trace
minerals, major deficiencies may develop. Lack of either
will make it impossible for the body to maintain good
health and function properly. In clay, the minerals occur
in natural proportion to one another, encouraging their
absorption in the intestinal tract. Natural Calcium
Montmorillonite restores minerals in the tissues where
they are needed. Furthermore, minerals are carriers of
the electrical potential in the cells which enable the
hormones, vitamins, and enzymes to function properly.[20]

Clay detoxifies by adsorbing and absorbing
Clay is a remarkably potent detoxifier, when applied externally or
when eaten. How does clay help detoxify? All toxins are positively
charged. Clay has negative ions. Thus, the clay's negative ions attract the
positively charged toxic matter, facilitating the movement of toxins
through the kidneys or the lymphatic system to a site of normal excretion.
This quality to attract toxic matter (due to negative electrical charge) is
called adsorption. Once attracted, the toxins are absorbed into the layers
of clay molecules and held together till dispelled from the body as waste.
This is why clay is so effective in poisoning and gastro-intestinal
disorders.

Scientific research gives evidence that bentonite can absorb
pathogenic viruses, aflatoxin (a mold), other pesticides and herbicides.[21]

Clay is holistic and active
Clay is an active agent that works intelligently. It withdraws the
infection from the body and fortifies the organism by acting on our
general metabolism. Even if you apply clay in one area for one particular
ailment, it will act on the whole body and heal other infections and
maladies that the patient is not even aware of.

What is it that makes clay intelligent and gives it its miraculous
powers of healing?

As mentioned earlier, many cultures revere the earth as a
representation of the mother due to its fecundity and its regenerative
powers. It decomposes but also gives life. The other elements that heal and
complete the cosmic balance are air, water and fire. Often naturopaths have
used a combination of these elements for healing. A mix of hydrotherapy,
yoga for breathing and curing, and eating the right food or fasting, has
helped cure ailments from ancient times. Gandhiji used a permutation of
clay, fasting and experimenting with different combinations of food for cure.

Clay contains all the elements. It is dried in the sun, mixed with
water and interacts with air. Thus, it is charged with all the elements. This
combination exercises a far greater force of healing – it is energy in its
primal and potent form. Its healing power is not just multi-fold but also
exponential. This, perhaps, is a more acceptable explanation as there is no
exact answer as to how clay heals all ailments so efficaciously.

Clay regenerates
The regenerative powers of clay are best exemplified when there
is an open wound. The manner in which it heals the skin tissues, often
without leaving the slightest scar, is nothing short of miraculous. Clay is
known to revive the metabolism of the body and even form new blood
corpuscles.

Clay is anti-inflammatory
Application of clay reduces swelling, whether internal or external.
In cases of external swelling, clay can be directly applied on the affected

area. In case of an internal injury, external applications are beneficial in
reducing both pain and inflammation.

Clay is an antiseptic
Clay also acts as an antiseptic in cases of wounds and injuries. It eliminates all bacteria and infection. If applied immediately, clay is sufficient. You don't even need a tetanus injection.

Kaolin was used:
for disinfection of the surgeon's hands before operation, where thorough rubbing of the hands with purified kaolin will — it is believed — remove all septic infection from the skin without causing the irritation of the skin so common with the use of the usual surgical antiseptics![22]

Clay acts on a virus
Unlike antibiotics that have no effect on a virus, clay is a potent resource that boosts the immune system of the body and helps it overcome the virus or viruses.

Clay provides protective coating
When applied on the skin or when taken internally, clay covers the injured area and protects it from outside aggression. For example, in cases of burns, the coating that is provided by clay prevents the oxidation process of the flesh and thus removes the pain caused by the burn. The *Indian Materia Medica* mentions that clay provides mechanical protective coating of the acutely inflamed gut.[23]

Clay acts on bacteria
It is interesting to note that clay has been used historically as an effective antibacterial in the treatment of dysentery, and as a means of decontaminating water. It appears that:
Presently it is being used internationally to clarify and balance small and large bodies of water. This is so because 'Living Clay' particles are smaller than many bacteria; when bacteria encounters an environment abundant in clay it becomes surrounded by the clay, and imbedded in it. The immediate result is that the bacteria are unable to receive nourishment and cannot survive.[24]

HOLISTIC VIEW ON THERAPY

There are several 'alternative' therapies that are popular. The scope of naturopathy is those forms of healing that a layperson can adopt. As mentioned earlier, the aim is to become independent and gain control over one's body, without recourse to specialists and organized systems.

Remaining in a state of good health implies a proper diet and lifestyle. It is highly recommended to people who desire to resort to naturopathy to adopt a vegetarian diet. This has been a point of debate with most people, as we touch upon a very sensitive issue: food. The adage 'we are what we eat' is apt. Our body reflects what we consume and influences the way we think. This is one of the messages of Ayurveda, the ancient Indian system of medicine, as defined in the *Charaka Samhita*.

There has been a revival of keen interest in vegetarian diets, though what constitutes vegetarian fare remains debatable. Here, by vegetarian, we mean including diary products but excluding eggs, meat and fish.

Having stated the importance of a vegetarian diet, it is relevant to note that food is classified into categories based on the qualities they possess and, thus, the qualities they induce.

A vegetarian diet
Of course the philosophical reason is that we do not kill animals or take life. Non-vegetarians often argue that even plants have life. True, so let us eat frugally and kill as little as we can. Whereas eating vegetables for survival is essential, killing an animal is not.

The other reason is that the human intestine is extremely long. This is a phenomenon existing in herbivorous animals. Food particles take

a long time to transit through the intestine. If the particles of food happen
to be that of meat, it will lead to putrefaction, as flesh decays more rapidly
and drastically than vegetables or fruits. This phenomenon is aggravated
when the food that is digested faster is slowed down by the presence of
food that is digested gradually. For example, if one has eaten bread first
and then some meat, as the cereal takes longer to transit, it will slow down
the transit of the meat that follows. This could probably be the reason why
a good many non-vegetarians suffer from diseases of the colon.

A healthy person digests food easily due to a healthy colon. Clay
is important as it assists the colon as a cleanser and gastro-intestinal
regulator.

At the end of the food chain, all food is converted into a kind of
protein. Eating vegetarian food means that our bodies will try and directly
absorb proteins and nutrients from the food. In the case of meat, one
consumes flesh that has already converted food into protein. In terms of
economy this is less desirable.

Vegetarian diet takes longer to digest and provides energy that is
longer lasting. A non-vegetarian diet is digested quicker and provides
immediate energy. The food we eat depends on what we want to do with
our lives. Do we wish to participate in a short 100 metre race and soon
get exhausted or run a life-long, energetic marathon? Having stated the
importance of a vegetarian diet, it is important to note that food is
classified into categories based on the qualities they possess and thus the
qualities they induce.

Hipbath
In his autobiography, Gandhiji dwells at length on the merits of
hydrotherapy, notably the hipbath as advocated by Kuhne. According to
this method, the patient should sit in a tub of cool water, immersing the
abdomen and the buttocks while keeping the feet outside. A plank in the
tub can serve as the headrest and portions of the body outside should be
well covered. While immersed in water, the abdomen should be rubbed
gently with a piece of cloth. The bath can last five to fifteen minutes. After
the bath, the patient should be dried and put to bed. A hipbath is
efficacious in reducing high fever. It appears to also help in cases of
constipation and improves digestion.

Enema

Washing the intestines by administering an enema is a quick way to eliminate accumulated toxins in the body. A few drops of castor oil can be added if the patient suffers from constipation. If there is infection or pain in the intestines, a spoonful of clay dissolved in water is very effective. As an enema can weaken the body, care should be taken in cases where the patient is already feeling weak.

Fasting

The effectiveness of a fast as a quick way to recovery is well known. By fasting, one directs the energy that is normally utilized in digestion to overcome the disease. Animals are known to stop eating when ill. Though fond of food, Gandhiji fasted often to cure himself of diverse ailments. It is, of course, difficult to adopt as the main therapy. A liquid diet is important as the body can dehydrate. Moreover, one has to take care to gradually stop eating solids and then to take small portions when one restarts.

Rest

It is important to take sufficient rest. Often, ailing people ignore their body and take painkillers and anti-inflammatory pills so that they can continue with their commitments. The body is put under unnecessary pressure till it becomes too late.

Rest, therefore, if taken properly and on time, will certainly save us from future complications.

Acupressure / Shiatsu

Acupressure provides immediate relief. For some types of acute pain it can be very useful and supplement clay therapy. Another person can impart acupressure but it is often quite easy to do it on one's own with the help of a chart locating the few main pressure points.

Oil massage

Massage is an ancient Ayurvedic tradition. This is still prevalent in India, though mostly for pregnant women, newborn babies and wrestlers. Oil massage became a dying tradition till a renewed interest in Ayurveda revived it, especially in Kerala. A good massage stimulates blood circulation and if combined with good quality herbal oil, is extremely beneficial.

OTHER USES OF CLAY

Cosmetic
Clay is used for many cosmetic preparations, notably for face masks. Green clay is used for oily skins and acne. Yellow clay is used for its cooling properties. White clay is used on dry skins. All the different types of clay are extremely beneficial as purifiers. They lighten the skin and remove impurities. Clay is also used in combination with different oils, creams and essences.

Clay mixed in water can be used for washing hair. This strengthens the hair roots and provides necessary minerals to the scalp.

Pale or yellow Ochre (Indian bazaar: *Multani mati*) is used externally in combination with fresh lemon juice and oil or curd and rose water for rubbing and washing head, which remove dandruff, softens the hairs, and keeps the head cool.[25]

Clay is an excellent toothpowder. Use powdered and purified clay. The clay should be so fine that it dissolves when you put it in your mouth. Mint leaves or other herbs can be mixed to give a refreshing flavour.

Psychological and therapeutic
It is common practice to encourage children to play with clay at school and at home. Children love to manipulate clay. The fact that plasticine or artificial play dough has replaced earthen clay is lamentable. Clay is malleable, can take any form, be reused and is completely safe. Clay helps children exercise their hand muscles, develop motor skills and also fosters creative talent. It is extremely beneficial for disturbed children who need to vent their frustration. Moreover, clay can be applied directly in case of psychological disorders such as neurosis. We have already

described how this type of treatment was used successfully in different parts of the world.

Clay or mud baths

Soaking oneself in a tub of prepared clay is also a practice in some health centres in India. Lying for a very long in a mud bath may, however, tire the body, so it is not advisable to initially soak in a clay bath alone. As mentioned earlier, mud baths are given to patients suffering from rheumatism in Thalassotherapy centres in France. In India, mud baths are administered to patients in naturopathy centres, the most famous being *Urli Kanchan* near Pune. Gandhiji himself initiated this centre.

Lifestyle

Clay pottery is commonly used in India. Water is stored in earthen jars made of red clay that contains a good deal of iron. These jars not only cool the water but also fortify it with minerals. Thus, clay pots are a natural refrigerator, aesthetic and beneficial for health. This tradition continues in India despite modernization and families that have a refrigerator continue to store water in jars called *matka* in Hindi.

SOME MYTHS AND MISCONCEPTIONS

It takes longer to be cured with clay
This depends on the nature of the ailment, how long the individual has been suffering and what medication has been taken.

Recovery can be extremely fast with clay. Yet, sometimes, the cure may take several months if the disease is deeply ingrained. However, clay therapy is holistic and in the long run a better option than just temporarily subduing the symptoms and carrying the disease for a lifetime. A minor and innocuous looking sore on the body may take weeks or months to heal with clay. This is probably because the body harbours a serious ailment that has found an outlet through this sore. On the other hand, there are cases where a chronic ailment may be cured within a few hours.

An acquaintance, who was a complete sceptic on clay therapy, once stayed with us. She suddenly developed conjunctivitis. Her eyes became very red and she panicked. A clay application was put on her arm. She grumbled about how cumbersome and dirty the process was, how ugly the bandage looked, that she should have been more careful when visiting this part of the country (she was a foreign national) as she had a chronic tendency to acquire conjunctivitis. With two applications, her eyes became normal and she left in the morning quite dazed with her rapid recovery without any medicine. She left, irrevocably tamed!

Those who use clay have a higher tolerance level of pain
This myth is completely untrue. Clay is such a great pain reliever that it is sad to see people suffer side effects of medicines and develop dependency on chemical drugs for relief. Clay is quick, effective and has no side effects. What naturopaths have is greater perseverance and a high degree of alertness to their bodies. For cases such as burns or painful ailments such as sciatica or zona, clay is perhaps the quickest pain

reliever. The pain returns only when you remove the clay application and if you maintain too long a gap between applications.

You believe in it, so it works

It is not so much a matter of belief as of persistence. If you apply it properly and regularly and there is no interference in terms of other drugs, clay will cure. There is nothing such as a placebo effect with the clay. It is possible for someone who does not believe in clay therapy to apply clay regularly on a patient. What is important is that the clay should be of good quality and it should be properly and regularly applied.

It is cumbersome

It is true that clay applications can be cumbersome, especially when applied on the lower back, stomach or other areas that restrict mobility. But then this is relative. Being in pain and suffering from an ailment is far more cumbersome. Most people who use clay regularly actually manage to continue their daily routine and professional lives.

It is dirty

Clay leaves no stains. It can be easily wiped or washed with just plain water.

Using clay makes my ailment worse

An ailment will appear to worsen, especially when there is a cut or an open wound. This is only because clay attracts the toxins through that infected channel on which it had been applied. Continue using clay in cases of open wounds without hesitation. In other cases, you may apply clay on another part of the body such as the arm to divert the flow of toxins.

It is addictive

You cannot become addicted to clay. There are no withdrawal symptoms! You have the option to stop using clay any time and resume the treatment whenever you want. It is, of course, better to continue till the disease disappears and a complete recovery is attained.

CLAY THERAPY:
SOME TESTIMONIES

General immunity, migraines, typhoid

I am a French national. Five years ago, I moved to India and had the privilege to live with the authors of the book. I was introduced to clay as a cure for all kinds of ailments and have been using it as my primary remedy ever since. In the process of acclimating myself to this new environment, I encountered problems like indigestion and frequent coughs and colds, all of which I would treat with clay. I have since reflected on the use of naturopathy versus allopathy. Naturopathy both requires and allows a person to be aware of one's own body in a way that allopathy does not. Because of the natural healing of clay, the body's immune system is not further disrupted by chemicals, instead it purges the ailment by attuning itself to its needs, thus becoming stronger along the way. I have been suffering from recurring migraines since I was young, it was only after using clay that I was able to identify the source of my headaches—lack of sleep or anxiety. Thus instead of curing the symptoms, I began to cure the problem. Previously, I would take an aspirin and keep on going, ignoring my body's warning signs, to either calm down, or get some sleep. Two years ago, I was down with typhoid, and confined to my bed for two weeks. During this time, I used clay intensively, and made a very speedy recovery given the seriousness of the ailment. I felt especially fortunate after a friend of mine was hospitalized with the same illness, and ended up on heavy antibiotics. It took her two and half months to get over it.

Most people in France know of clay only as a facial product. Interestingly I came to find out that my father had used clay as a medicinal tool in the early 70s. More astonishing was the use of clay by my grandmother. After she gave birth to my father in 1950, she developed an abscess on her breast. She consulted several specialists in Paris who said the only way to proceed was to operate. Her repulsion to the idea led her to try clay as a last resort. In a matter of days, the abscess disappeared, and never returned. My father is now a wandering Buddhist monk living in remote monasteries in Myanmar (Burma). My father visited me in India and seeing a community of people successfully using clay as a cure, he was inspired to restart his own clay cures. His close-to-nature lifestyle exposes him to many tropical parasites and illnesses that are found in the thick forests and jungles of Myanmar. Using clay, he has cured not only himself but several other monks in the monasteries that he visits. Aside from curing tropical fevers, indigestions and bacterial infections, he also uses it for psoriasis with notable success. He finds clay in nature and refines it himself before using it.

I have noticed that the strongest resistance to clay and other natural remedies often comes from people who derive their identity from their poor health—either to draw attention or to withdraw from life's many challenges, never mind the fact that these patients only experience temporary relief out of their medicinal treatments. What appeals to me in the natural approach to healing is the feeling of being empowered to take control of my own health, instead of putting my fate entirely in someone else's hands. Besides, the complexity and interdependence within the body still eludes the most advanced medical practitioners, so how much do we really know? We can never ascertain the full impact of an allopathic medication. I believe that nature knows more than science ever will. The human body has evolved with nature for millennia; in the long run, the body will react and adjust better to a natural stimulus than an artificial one. One of the key ingredients in using clay or any medicine for that matter is conviction; we must feel that we are healing ourselves through our actions.

Benjamin Mailian, 25 years, teacher

Typhoid, malaria, chronic cold

I am nineteen years old. Since birth I haven't had any allopathic medicines. I have suffered from malaria, typhoid, mumps, skin irritations, sinus outbreaks and conjunctivitis but, each time, I cured myself with clay applications.

I was in Nepal when I contracted typhoid. My father cancelled an important meeting abroad and rushed to me in the nick of time to ensure I was restored to health with clay therapy. I applied clay as usual on my arm for a few days, but felt an irritation, instead, on my right knee. So I began applying clay there. To everyone's surprise, my knee began releasing pus from a wound. As days went by, the lesion widened and deepened, to the extent that we could see my bone with the naked eye. Everyone was aghast but my father ensured that my clay treatment remained uninterrupted. Relatives were worried and wanted me to switch over to allopathic medicines. They didn't believe in clay and thought it was madness to continue. But I am glad my father stood up to the opposition. Once the toxins were flushed out, the wound began to heal. It took around ten days for complete cure. Today, I have no scars on my knee and I have never had another attack of typhoid.

In less than two days, clay cured me of a deadly version of malaria, which hits the brain. I was ten years old then. I applied clay and was healed so quickly that I could resume going to school within four days. Many of my classmates who suffered from the same malady and took recourse to regular allopathic medicines were absent for at least fifteen to twenty days and continued to suffer from bouts of weakness thereafter.

In 1997, I caught a cold just before my semester exams. I thought I should try some other cure, as clay would make me lose time. I tried an off-the-shelf medicated syrup that promised to clear my congested nose for twelve hours at a stretch. Having taken it, I went happily to give my exams. Believe it or not, I had to write my paper with a handkerchief covering my nose! My body reacted badly to the medicated syrup and began producing phlegm in large quantities to eject the medicine I had taken. I still didn't believe clay would heal me and continued various other options like homeopathy, Ayurveda and home remedies. Ultimately, I had to resort to clay therapy as no other treatment gave me respite. The cold took a month and a half to heal and it was a nightmare. Since then I have had recurrent bouts of cold but by then I knew that the only way for me to feel better was to apply clay on my nose. If I had to attend school or undertake other tasks, I would apply clay on my upper arm and try acupressure on the sinus points located on my face and in my hands. I tried to understand what triggered off these colds – for me it is dust and pollution. Today, thanks to clay therapy I am completely healed of this problem.

If you intend to start clay therapy, I suggest you:
- Be persistent and continue till the illness is gone. Apply mud

even when working, sleeping.

- Don't wait for the illness to be full-blown. Attack it at the root as soon as the symptoms threaten. This way, you heal faster and for good.
- Keep a positive frame of mind and believe that you will heal. In other words, behave as normally as possible. If you keep thinking you are ill, you will eventually fall sick.
- Listen to your body.
- Be patient. The healing will take its own time, whether you want it to or not.

Today I work, I listen to my body and take care of myself. Most importantly, I try to cure myself with clay before the illness gets the better of me!

Lissa Chazot, 19 years, student

Glass in the foot, thumb injury

I was working in the kitchen when a Pyrex casserole broke and fell on the floor. As I was holding another hot dish, I happened to step on the splintered glass and injured my foot. The shards pierced my foot and the injured area rapidly turned dark blue. I applied a lot of clay on the entire spot. Within twenty-four hours, after three or four applications, my foot was much better. When I removed the clay, I found pieces of glass, along with pus and infection. So I reapplied clay and wrapped my foot in a large cloth bandage. This permitted me to hop around a bit. When I wobbled around, I could feel something sharp still lurking in the injured area. It did not hurt but I could feel the glass.

Then, a few days later, the most amazing thing happened. A hole appeared at the sole of my foot and small pieces of glass continued to be sucked out onto the clay. This did not prevent me from walking, nor did it give me any great discomfort. When all the pieces of glass had been thus removed, the hole closed on its own and healed completely. As my wound and the manner of dressing it was unusual, most people around me were scared and thought I would lose my foot or would have to go in for an operation.

Clay also cured me of chronic rheumatism.

I was once peeling a very thick gourd with a sharp knife that slipped and sliced my thumb to the bone. I immediately applied clay. The wound bled for nearly twenty-four hours but I continued with my work. Over a period of time, my thumb healed completely and there was no loss in terms of movement or agility.

Jacqueline Chazot, 74 years, housewife

Sciatica, arthritis

Very often I had been suffering from sciatica. The throbbing was so acute that I would be bed-ridden on some occasions. This would make me resort to anti-inflammatory drugs and injections. I discovered clay when I was fifty-five and started clay applications when my pain became unbearable. After a few days I felt completely fit. So I discontinued the applications. Whenever I had long days or exerted myself, my pain would return and back I would go to clay therapy for relief. Now, five years later, I have had no relapses and even sleeping on a soft bed does not induce any distress as it used to do in the past.

I also started suffering from arthritis. My knees gave me great trouble and the doctors advised an operation in order to remove water from my knee. As I did not want to undergo surgery, I started applying clay on my knees at night. I continued with the treatment for a month, with two applications during the day and one at night. I have been cured of arthritis in a few weeks' time and what is more important, this affliction has not returned to plague me ever again. Now I lead an active life, travelling and meeting my family, much to their surprise and, I think, envy!

Prem Kanta Musafir, 60 years, businesswoman

Viral fever, back injury

I am 14 years old and study in Mahatma Gandhi International School. That's where I came to know about clay therapy. It's like a miracle cure. When I first came to know about it, I didn't believe it. But as I started learning more about the miraculous powers of clay from some of my teachers, I thought I would also try it. I had been watching them put clay whenever they were not feeling well, and the next day they would be at school, completely fresh and with no signs of illness.

I have been taking different kinds of medicines right from the time I was born. I always hated them. But, I like clay, and look forward to applying it because it makes me feel nice and cool. I love to use it, especially during summers, as I feel calm and relaxed.

I have been applying clay for six months now, and I am extremely happy with the result. Once, during high fever, I applied only clay. In the beginning I was not very confident. But I had seen my teacher use it to good effect. So I gave it a try too. I was well in two days. I only had to miss one day of school. By the third day I was back on the courts, playing tennis!

Once, during a session of long jumps in school, I fell on a hard surface. The injury on my back was so bad that I couldn't even sit properly on a chair. I collapsed due to acute pain. But in one and a half days' time I was back on my feet, thanks to clay.

As soon as I became thirteen, I started to get pimples. But, again, clay applications made them do the vanishing act. I do not get acne any longer. Of course, it took some time but the cure was holistic.

I had never in my wildest dreams thought that just a handful of clay had so much power to heal. After watching me use clay, my parents and my grandmother have also become converts. The best thing about clay is that it can cure anything; you name it and clay can cure it. That's magic!

Sunaina Shah, 14 years, student

Burns
I was cooking in the kitchen and had just boiled some milk. The gas was next to an open window in my ground floor apartment. Some children were playing cricket outside. I had told the boys not to hit the ball hard when one of them went in for a stylish shot. The ball, alas, landed on the gas and spilt the boiling milk right on my foot. I sustained third degree

burns. Hearing my screams, some neighbours came running. They applied ice and cold water. My foot became swollen and I had large blisters. Everyone was sure I would not be able to walk for at least a month. My husband works at Darpana Academy and Mallika Sarabhai, on hearing of my accident, sent some clay (white *gopi chandan*). I did not know how to use it so I simply applied it as a paste on the injury. This was soothing and cooling and provided relief. I then learnt that I was to apply it as a poultice. I did so and within twenty-four hours my blisters disappeared, leaving behind a very pink skin. In fifteen days I was totally cured and had not the slightest scar. Visitors cannot believe I had such an accident and those who had seen my state marvel at this treatment.

Mrs. Unnati Hemant Trivedi, 45 years, housewife

Diabetes

The sky fell on my head the day my blood report arrived. As part of routine check-up for my insurance policy, my total health profile was done. Being a doctor, I thought I was in perfect shape. To my utter horror, I turned out to be a heavy diabetic. My fasting blood sugar was 210 mg (normal is upto 110) and my post lunch sugar was 370 mg (normal is upto 140). I went to the diabetologist and said I was prepared to do anything to get back to normal. I certainly did not want to be on lifelong medications. He gave me fifteen days to try whatever I wanted and then return to him.

I had heard about clay therapy from Anjou and Pascal. I knew about its immense power to cure. With complete trust I rushed to them and they were extremely cooperative. I learnt to apply clay round the clock. They gave the initial stock. Later, I replenished it. I administered the clay applications religiously. After just eleven days I checked my sugar count and to my great astonishment, the fasting count was 114 and post-lunch count had come down to 119. Believe it or not, I was free from diabetes. I had not just controlled it but cured myself completely. I might have helped thousands of patients with my medical skill, but I cannot forget that I have got a new lease of life with the help of clay. I believe without any doubt that many medical problems can be solved, if clay is used with dedication and persistence.

Ajay Sinha (named changed on request), 38 years, doctor

ENDNOTES

1   Nadkarni, *Indian Materia Medica*, 7, 8.
2   Dextreit, *L'argile qui guérit, memento de médecine naturelle.*
3   *Indian Medical Gazette*, February 1926.
4   Nadkarni, *Indian Materia Medica*, 94.
5   Gandhi, *Nature Cure*, 7, 8.
6   In our experience, heating clay as Gandhi describes it, as well as mixing it with oil reduces the healing properties and hence its efficiency, sometimes drastically.
7   Gandhi, *Nature Cure*.
8   McDermott and O' Connor, *NLP and Health*.
9   Valnet, *Aromathérapie, traitement des maladies par les essences de plantes*, 76, 77.
10 Gandhi, *Harijan*.
11 Nadkarni, *Indian Materia Medica*, 7.
12 Ibid., 94.
13 Laing and Esterson, *Sanity, Madness and the Family*.
14 http://www.shirleys-wellness-cafe.com/
15 *Times of India*, July 14, 2003.
16 Nadkarni, *Indian Materia Medica*, 10.
17 Ibid., 9.
18 Dextreit, *L'argile qui guérit, memento de médecine naturelle.*
19 Nadkarni, *Indian Materia Medica*, 7.
20 http://www.shirleys-wellness-cafe.com/
21 *Canadian Journal of Microbiology* 31 (1985): 50–53.
22 Nadkarni, *Indian Materia Medica*, 9.
23 Ibid.
24 http://www.shirleys-wellness-cafe.com/
25 Nadkarni, *Indian Materia Medica*, 10, 11.

WHERE TO PURCHASE CLAY

AUSTRALIA
The Clay Company
2029 Rose Bay
argile1@lprimus.com.au

BELGIUM
Strath
3 Rue Pré Colin
6120 Jamioulx
naturalia@skynet.be

BENIN
La Sante Par Les Aliments
BP 307
Cotonou
jeanpliya@yahoo.fr

CAMEROON
Tcla'diet
BP 3936
Douala

CANADA
Argiletz Canada
Centre D'affaire Longueuil
663 Bld JP Vincent
QC J4G 1R3
Longueuil
argiletz@qc.aira.com

CYPRUS
Pambos Efstathiou
168 Ellados Str.
Limassol

FINLAND
Vertim Oy
Jokitie 3
1800 Klaukkala

FRANCE
Available in all Medical shops (Pharamcie)
on order
Also available in shops selling organic
food products (Magasins Dietetiques)

For organic clay:
GASSENDI
Dietetique Boite N°1
23–25, Rue Gassendi
75014 Paris
http://www.biorganic.ifrance.com

ARGILETZ
14 Route D'echampeau
77 440 Lizy Sur Ourcq
France
Phone: 01 60 61 20 88
Fax: 01 60 61 27 39
info@argiletz.com

French Overseas Regions:
GUADELOUPE
Energy Sante
BP 362
97096 St Barthelemy

MARTINIQUE
Dietetique Plus
157 Rue Moreau De Gounes
97200 Fort De France

Diedis
Les Hauts De Californie
97232 Le Lamentin
diedis@outremer.com

REUNION ISLAND
Biodet
25 Avenue De La Victoire
97464 St Denis Cedex

Diet Sante
51 Rue Du Commerce
97460 Saint Paul

GERMANY
Bachert
An Der Obermuhle 3–5
65719 Hofheim A TS

Jatex
Hammerwerkstr.9
D7632 Pfinztal
mail@terranatura.de

GREAT BRITAIN
Lydia Ltd
PO Box 18 Cardigan
SA43 3YH Wales
info@lydia@ltd.uk

GREECE
Biotopos
53 Frangopoulos Street
14561 Kifissia

HOLLAND
Aroma Vera
Steurstraat 55
1317 NX Almere
armin@aromavera.nl

INDIA
Vijnana
Auroville, Pondicherry, Tamil Nadu
http://www.auroville.com/vijnana

ITALY
Docteur Nature
6/12 Via Caduti Senza Croce
41041 Baggiovara

IVORY COAST (REPUBLIC OF)
Maison Dietetique
04 BP 1053
Abidjan 04

JAPAN
Aromafrance
24-11-301 Kosobe-Cho
1 Chome
Takatsuki 569-1115
argile-japon@store.email.ne.jp

KOREA
C.A.H.A.
419 Daechi-3 Dong
Kangnam Gu
Seoul

LUXEMBOURG
Naturvita
4 Rue Des Joncs
1818 Howald

NETHERLANDS
Chi International BV
Koele Mei 2
4816 JD Breda

NORWAY
Cosmodermica
Nedre Storgt 45
3015 Drammen

MK Konsult
Gardemoveien 81
2050 Jessheim

Biovital Norge
PB 63 Hauketo
1206 Oslo

POLAND
Arpol
Ui Kochanowskiego 12/30
1864 Warszawa
arpol-fr@atj.pl

SPAIN
Prod'sitges
Pilar Franquet 4 6
8870 Sitges Barcelone

Farma Serra Mandri
Rue Diagonale 478
8006 Barcelone
farma@farmaciaserra.com

SWEDEN
Crearome AB
Jarnvagspatan 18
59430 Gamleby

Sanna Nature
Rimfrostragen 16
69152 Kariskoga

SWITZERLAND
Schild
Chemin De Jolimont 12
2300 La Chaux De Fonds

Willemin Et Rebetez
Avenue De La Gare 38
2800 Delemont

Cedis Nature
8 Rue Cavour
1211 Geneve 13

Mat'horse
Ru Du Four 29
1401 Yvernon Les Bains

TOGO
La Promaico
BP 838
97 Boulevard Circulaire
Lom

UNITED STATES OF AMERICA
Cedarvale Natural Health Inc,
P.O. Box 575
Cedarvale
Kansas 67024
Tel: 866 758 1012

Interesting websites on clay:

www.shirleys-wellness-cafe.com

www.eytonsearth.org

www.wholisticresearch.com

For an update on clay usage and
purchase, check the website
www.idealfoundation.com/clay

BIBLIOGRAPHY

Canadian Journal of Microbiology 31 (1985): 50–53.

Dalet, Roger. *Supprimez vous meme vos douleurs par simple pression d'un doigt.* Paris: Edition de Trévise, 1978.

Dextreit, Raymond. *L'argile qui guérit, memento de médecine naturelle.* France: Editions Vivre en harmonie, 1997.

Gandhi, M. K. *The Selected Works of Mahatma Gandhi,* 6 vols. Ahmedabad: Navajivan Publishing House, 1968.

———. *Nature Cure.* 1954. Ahmedabad: Navajivan Publishing House, 1997.

———. *Key to Health.* 1948. Ahmedabad: Navajivan Publishing House, 1996.

Goodrich, Janet. *Bien voir sans lunettes.* Paris: Terre Vivante, 1993.

Groddeck, Georg. *Le livre du ça.* Paris: Gallimard, 1973.

Indian Medical Gazette, February 1926.

Kakar, Sudhir. *Shamans, Mystics and Doctors.* New York: Knopf, 1982.

McDermott, Ian and Joseph O'Connor. *NLP and Health.* London: Thorsons, 2001.

Nadkarni, K. M. *Indian Materia Medica.* Bombay: Bombay Popular Prakashan, 1976.

Sayadaw, Pa-Auk, *Mindfulness of Breathing and Four Elements Meditation.* Kuala Lumpur: Wave, 1999.

Sengupta, Kaviraj. *The Ayurvedic System of Medicine,* vols. 1 and 2. Delhi: Sri Satguru Publications, 1998.

Stein, Diane. *The Natural Remedy Book for Women.* Delhi: Sri Satguru Publications, 1992.

Tulku, Thondup. *The Healing power of Mind.* Boston & London: Shambhala, 1996.

Valnet, Jean. *Aromathérapie, traitement des maladies par les essences de plantes.* Paris: Maloine S. A. éditeur, 1976.

Vanhowten, Donald. *Ayurveda & Life Impressions Bodywork.* Delhi: Motilal Banarsidass Publishers Pvt. Ltd., 1998.

INDEX

ACKNOWLEDGEMENTS

The idea to pen our experiences was inspired by Mrs. Mrinalini Sarabhai. We would like to thank her for her constant support and reminders that spurred us to see this book through.

We specially thank all our friends and family members who themselves are now adept users of clay and who shared their experiences in this book. We also thank Sarvodaya International Trust that seeks to promote Gandhian ideals and philosophy. This book is part of an initiative of the Sarvodaya International Trust, Gujarat Chapter.